EXTREME
SPORTS

IN SEARCH OF THE ULTIMATE THRILL

THIS IS A CARLTON BOOK

Text and design © 1996, 2001, 2004 Carlton Books Limited

First published in 1996

A CIP catalogue record for this book is available from the British Library

ISBN 1 84442 708 0

Printed in Dubai

Editor: Nigel Matheson
Project art direction: James Locoweed
Production: Lisa French

PICTURE ACKNOWLEDGMENTS
The publishers would like to thank the following sources for their kind permission to reproduce the pictures in this book:

Agencie DPPI: /F Clement: 164, 165; **Bluewater Freedivers:** /Terry Maas: 131, 140/141, 162, 163; **Brad McDonald:** 62, 64, 65; **Buzz Pictures:** 141; /John Carter: 190-191; /Danny Fitzpatrick: 139r; /Nick Hamilton: 123; /Neale Haynes: 21, 48t, 56, 63, 67b, 73, 74, 98, 99tr, 100, 111b, 122, 124r, 125, 133, 142; /Adam Kola: 59b, 59t, 60t; /Dean O'Flaherty: 8, 9bl, 34, 35, 39, 40, 41; /John McGillicuddy: 18-19, 20; /Jon Nash: 153; /Sean Richards: 7, 13; /Leo Sharp: 108-9, 111t; /Russ Shea: 99br; /Geoff Waugh: 48br, 91, 92-93b, 92-93t, 93, 94-5, 97; /Ray Wood: 102, 103; /Chris Woodage: 66b, 67t; **Cleva:** Colorsport: 19; /Fotosports International: 78-79 ,80l, 80r, 81, 82, 83, 84b, 85; /Tony Harrington/Sporting Pictures: 47, 76; /Stefan Hunziker: 115; /Brett Stanley: 107l, 109, 175t; /Sporting Pictures: 4-5, 6, 38-39, 46, 64, 66t, 107r, 118, 120, 121, 131, 175b, 177, 177-178; **Corbis Images:** 146-147; /Stephen Frink: 158; /Gideon Mendel: 136; /Picimpact: 71; /Larry Williams: 161; **Empics:** 49, 84t, 113, 132; / Shelly Castellano: 61; / Grant Ellis/Zuma Press: 172; /Chris McLennan: 118-119; /Jan-Peter Kasper/DPA: 75; /Sportschrome: 112, 116-117; /Zuma Press: 170-171, 174; **Getty Images/ALLSPORT:** 26, 86, 87, 148/149, 156; /Kurt Amsler: 153 right, 158, 159, 160, 161; /Nathan Bilow: 52, 53, 54 bottom L, 55 right, 104 left; /Luciano Bosari: 151; /Simon Bruty: 24, 25, 128, 129; /B Buffet: 51; /Marc Cazals: 150 left; /Sylvain Cazenave: 178/179; /Gerard Ceccaldi: 134 bottom; /Stanley Chou: 60 bottom; /Bernard Desestres: 22, 23; /Vania Fine: 102 left; /JP Galtier: 72; /Lluis Gene/AFP: 146, 147; / Didier Givois: 70, 71, 104/105, 180/181; /Martti Kainulainen: 32; /Joe Klamar/AFP/: 9 bottom R; /Didier Klein: 38 left, 41 bottom; /JP Lenfant: 135; /Nigel Marple: 52 top; /Bob Martin: 52 bottom R; /Thierry Martinez: 152; /Robert Michael/AFP/: 33; /Remy Michelin: 58; /Stephen Munday: 154/155; /Gerard Planchenault: 68; /Adam Pretty: 54; /Alain Revel: 105 right; /Francois Rickard: 36,37; /Pascal Rondeau: 126, 149 mid; /William Sallaz: 149 top; /Brunel Sunergy: 154; /Pascal Tournaire: 77 right, 101; /Vandystadt: 14, 20, 21, 16, 34, 35, 149 bottom; /Anton Want: 50, 96 left, bottom; /Simon Ward: 36 left; **PA Photos:** EPA: 28, 29; **Phorum/Mark D. Phillips:** 29; **Polar:** 52bl; **Redbull:** Stefan Aufschnaiter: 138; /Ulrich Grill: 44, 44bl; /Francois Portmann: 130, 139l; Bernhard Spottel: 9tr, 10, 12, 43, 124l, 127; **Rex Features:** Zena Holloway: 140; /Stuart Martin: 157r; **Rocky Mountain:** 90; **Steb Fisher Photography:** 166l, 166r; **Stockfile/Steve Thomas:** 124, 125; **Topfoto.co.uk:** PressNet: 157m; **www.windjet.co.uk:** 88

Every effort has been made to acknowledge correctly and contact the source and/or copyright holder of each picture, and Carlton Books Limited apologises for any unintentional errors or omissions which will be corrected in future editions of this book.

EXTREME SPORTS

IN SEARCH OF THE ULTIMATE THRILL

JOE TOMLINSON with ED LEIGH

CARLTON
BOOKS

CONTENTS

INTRODUCTION

TEAM SPORTS ARE ON THE WANE AND A NEW BREED OF SPORTS IS TAKING THEIR PLACE. EXTREME SPORTS ARE ALL ABOUT ATTITUDE, INDIVIDUALITY AND, ABOVE ALL, PUSHING EVERYTHING TO THE LIMIT.

What are Extreme Sports all about? What is it that gets athletes charged up enough to put their lives at risk? Is it all just a big adrenaline fixation? I don't think so.

Which is not to say that there isn't a quest for an adrenaline charge in extreme sports—there is. Most athletes, however, who consider themselves to be extreme are not lunatics seeking a buzz no matter what the consequences may be.

They get their adrenal rush because their skills allow them to perform safely under conditions that are dangerous or even life-threatening. They can successfully do things that could kill those unfamiliar with their particular sports because they have dedicated themselves to performing within their limits, even while they have consistently challenged themselves to redefine what those limits are.

Extreme sports are about individuality, higher and higher levels of achievement, redefining performance boundaries, and the personal satisfaction that comes from trying your best. Extreme sports deliver a sense of accomplishment, whether you establish a new level of ability or simply challenge yourself while having a great time.

Extreme sports do not generally prohibit you from having fun because of your physical size or build, but they do require for you to be in shape. You can enjoy your sports without the threat of a 300-pound adversary slamming you to the ground or a competing eight-foot giant keeping you from your goal. What you are pitting yourself against in extreme sports, however, is a much less forgiving opponent, the Earth and its elements—air, land, and water. To challenge "mother nature" is far more formidable than competing with any individual.

There is a level of respect that should be afforded all extreme athletes, whether they are experts or beginners.

As the saying goes, "you have to be a kook sometime"—translation, you have to start somewhere. None of the extreme sports are easy enough for a first time attempt to be done well, or safely in some cases, without assistance or supervision. Extreme sports are passed down and across from athlete to athlete, and there is a true sense of satisfaction to be gained from introducing a newcomer to your extreme sport of choice.

The extreme sports movement has been quick to embrace the idea of the "crossover" athlete. Moving over from one extreme sport to another is encouraged. An expert snowboarder may find that mountain biking really turns them on, so they begin to develop their skills on a bike. That same snowboarder may also find that boardsailing is a thrill, and so begins the process of learning to boardsail.

The snowboarding, mountain biking, board-sailing athlete may then decide to try kiteboarding, hang gliding, climbing, kayaking, or any other number of extreme sports. As they build their repertoire of sports, they become better "crossover" athletes, and each extreme sport adds a little to their skills in other extreme sports by broadening their ideas on how things can be done.

How extreme sports have impacted on each other is really the story of the evolution of extreme sports until today. Some of the sports are very old, like bungee jumping. Some of the sports are more recent, like mountain-boarding. Both have elements that can be found in other extreme sports.

The thrill of freefall was first found in bungee, but it can be found in windsurfing, snowboarding, skiing, B.A.S.E jumping, etc. The joy of carving a turn on a mountain board is new, but it has its roots in surfing, skateboarding, wakeboarding, snowboarding, etc.

Extreme sports are about gravity, ingenuity, and technology. Gravity is the force that pulls climbers off rock faces, skiers down slopes and off cliffs, hang gliders toward the ground, and water downstream. Gravity makes warm air rise above cold, drives water to settle at the lowest available spot to create lakes and seas, creates the swirling mass of atmosphere that drives the winds. Gravity shaped our planet.

Ingenuity and technology are responsible for the multitude of ways we have discovered to use the forces of nature to enjoy nature. The evolution of extreme sports is a story of pushing available technologies and designs in order to improve performance. From high-tech fabrics to composite construction methods to innovations in design, extreme sports have evolved through the years thanks to the energies of many pioneers.

Extreme sports are exciting because they are full of energy and spirit. Of course, they are visually exciting, as the pictures throughout this book amply confirm. Most importantly, extreme sports have a life-affirming quality that stretches from the story of their evolution to the sheer pleasure they offer to those who participate at any level.

The world is a big place, with elements that offer plenty of challenges. Enjoy the planet and embrace the sports that celebrate being a part of it—extreme sports!

If you want to take your interest in any of these sports further, you should search the internet for activities and organizations in your area. Participate and have lots of fun!

THE EARTH AND ITS ELEMENTS—AIR, LAND AND WATER. THE WORLD IS A BIG PLACE WITH LOTS TO SEE AND DO. EXTREME SPORTS INVOLVE CHALLENGING MOTHER NATURE AND LIVING TO TELL THE TALE.

AIR SPORTS

IT'S FAIR TO SAY THAT SPORTS PERFORMED IN THE AIR ARE EXTREME. IT IS ALSO FAIR TO SAY THAT TAKING PART IN THESE SPORTS CAN BE EXTREMELY LIFE-THREATENING.

Imagine the consequences of a parachute that doesn't deploy or deploys only half way, a balloon that suddenly deflates, a glider caught in a violent downdraft, or a sky surfer spinning out of control. Air offers little resistance, so it can't keep the forces of gravity from drawing our bodies to the earth's surface. Only the drag created as objects pass through the air limits the speeds at which they travel down to earth. Another useful fact about the air that covers our planet is that it varies in temperature. Warm air rises until it cools in the upper atmosphere, and then it travels downward once again to the earth's surface. Here, it is warmed again, and the cycle is complete.

The air is much like an ocean, with its ever flowing tides and currents. Because the elements that make up the air are lighter than the ocean and the land, the air knows no borders. When it pushes up against land or sea, it simply follows the path of least resistance and moves on to pursue its intended direction. Understanding how air travels as it crosses the planet is of paramount importance to the creation and growth of extreme air sports.

We have discovered a number of ways to defy gravity in the air. First we used vines and cords. Then we made balloons, parachutes, and wings, and, using these to channel the air to create lift or sufficient drag to control the speed at which we fall to earth, we created sports that our ancestors could only dream about. Legendary Icarus was said to be the first to test the limits of flight only to perish in his famous tumble to earth after flying too close to the sun. Leonardo Da Vinci drafted many sketches after envisioning craft capable of flight, from the balloon to the helicopter. A few short decades ago, many of the techniques currently used to test the air could have only been imagined in the pages of Flash Gordon or a Jules Verne novel.

IT'S LONG BEEN THE DREAM OF MANKIND TO FLY LIKE THE BIRDS, AND NOW WE REALLY CAN. CLOCKWISE (LEFT TO RIGHT): SKY DIVING; BUNGEE JUMPING; SKY FLYING; SKI JUMPING; SKY SURFING.

The thrill of taking to the air like a bird, hurtling to earth at high speed only to float to a stop, is what has drawn athletes to push the limits of what is possible in the air. One can only imagine that early balloonists would have considered it insanity if anyone had suggested jumping from their craft attached to an elastic cord or a parachute. Of course, these original pioneers of aviation were then considered to be the crazy risk-takers for pursuing flight. They were the early extreme air sports enthusiasts. In time, they were forced to create vehicles, namely parachutes, that could allow them to escape their balloons with their lives if the worst were to occur. Soon items of necessity became ones of play, and the limits of air were again redefined.

Now athletes are surfing, flipping, gliding, and bouncing through the air in defiance of gravity. The opportunity to jump from aircraft is less than a century old. The first bungee jumpers used vines to break their fall to earth. There was a day when a high wire walk was a circus trick.

It is safe to assume that during the course of the next century, athletes will continue to redefine what can and can't be done in the air until what is cutting edge today becomes commonplace.

Right now we can feel satisfied that all of the currently defined limits are newly defined. In the years ahead new boundaries will be established and what is in these pages may become archaic. Either way, there is no question that the core emotion and andrenaline rush that comes from pushing the limits of what can be done in the air will remain, and athletes will continue probing and testing the boundaries of aerial extreme sports.

WHAT GOES UP MUST COME DOWN, BUT THERE'S NO NEED FOR ANYONE TO DESCEND TOO QUICKLY. CLOCKWISE (LEFT TO RIGHT): HIGH WIRE WALKING; B.A.S.E. JUMPING; HANG-GLIDING; GLIDING.

10

B.A.S.E. JUMPING

IF ANY OF THE EXTREME SPORTS CAN BE CONSIDERED TRULY HIGH RISK, THEN B.A.S.E. JUMPING IS IT. "B.A.S.E." IS AN ACRONYM FOR BUILDINGS, ANTENNA TOWER, SPAN, EARTH.

B.A.S.E. jumpers are athletes who leap from objects which fall under the categories B.A.S.E. represents. Generally these objects are not very high off the ground, and so the jumper must deploy his parachute very quickly or risk impacting the ground at deadly speed.

According to *The Skydiver's Handbook*, evidence exists that suggests B.A.S.E. jumping can be traced back as far as 900 years. Whether or not these jumpers survived to leap again is unknown. Modern B.A.S.E. jumping is believed to have started in 1978, when daring parachutists first began jumping off El Capitan, a 3,000 foot (915m) cliff high above Yosemite National Park. This site has remained a hotbed for U.S. B.A.S.E. jumpers.

The term B.A.S.E. was coined by B.A.S.E. pioneers Phil Smith and Jean Boenish. By January of 1981, the first four B.A.S.E. jumpers had completed jumps in all four B.A.S.E. categories, giving birth to the U.S. B.A.S.E. Association. As jumpers successfully complete all four categories, they receive their official B.A.S.E. number. Phil Smith of Houston, Texas is B.A.S.E. #1.

B.A.S.E. has an outlaw reputation in the U.S., and is illegal. There are several countries worldwide where B.A.S.E. is legal. Some of the better-known legal sites are in France, Norway, and Brazil. One of the most daring and highly publicized illegal jumps in the U.S.

was made by John Vincent of New Orleans, Louisiana. John climbed to the top of the Saint Louis Arch using suction cups as handholds, and jumped. John was later arrested by the FBI for jumping from a national monument, and spent 90 days in a federal prison. Jumps in the U.S. are now punishable by up to one year in jail and $5,000 (£3,000) fine.

Anyone considering becoming a B.A.S.E. jumper or doing any type of B.A.S.E. jump should have completed at least 100 skydives. B.A.S.E. jumpers must be extremely familiar and comfortable with their gear.

The jumper must have particularly strong freefall skills, as the ability to maintain correct body attitude during freefall is key to a safe deployment and landing.

The need for excellent canopy skills should not be underestimated. Obviously, a jumper whose chute doesn't open properly or immediately, must possess the skills necessary to open or redeploy the chute as quickly as possible, or that jump could well be their last.

The fundamental equipment used in B.A.S.E. jumping is the same as that used in parachuting. However, because B.A.S.E. jumping requires a much faster deployment, some of the traditional equipment must be modified. An example is the pilot chute, which is used to deploy the main parachute. Pilot chutes are always deployed by hand in a

13

DID HE JUMP OR WAS HE PUSHED? CLOCKWISE (LEFT TO RIGHT): FELIX BAUMGARTNER HALFWAY UP A B.A.S.E. JUMPING TOWER AT MESSINA; CHECK OUT HIS TECHNIQUE AS HE PLUNGES; IT'S NOT ALWAYS DONE TO TAKE THE ELEVATOR FROM THE TOP OF THE KL TOWER, KUALA LUMPUR.

B.A.S.E. jump. Depending on the distance of the freefall, the jumper may elect to hold the pilot chute in their hand or stow it in an easily accessible pocket on their pack. The jumper may also elect to use a small or large pilot chute depending on how quickly the main chute must be deployed. Some freefalls can be as small as 250 feet (76m), with only a few seconds separating the jump and any potential impact. Jumpers tend to use the hand deployment technique in short freefalls to reduce the potential for a missed pilot chute deployment and the resultant impact. Freefalls of 3,000 feet (915m), such as Angel Falls in Venezuela, can generally be made with the pilot chute stowed for deployment.

Different jumps require different types of main parachutes, otherwise referred to as the "canopy." The selection of the correct canopy is critical to ensuring a consistent and timely deployment. Most B.A.S.E. jumpers prefer wing-like "ram air" canopies. Ram air chutes deploy very rapidly and afford the jumper more control and steering precision than the traditional round canopies. Quick deployment and steerability are particularly important when jumping from objects like antennas, which are secured by high-tension wires, or cliffs, which may have sizeable outcroppings which must be avoided. Ram air canopies provide the jumper with a directional deployment, whereby the jumper can be sure of continuing their predeployed direction on deployment. Additionally useful is the ability to steer the canopy away from objects on the ground, such as a river...or waiting police. Therefore it is easy to understand how jumping off the Empire State Building can pose an entirely different set of challenges than jumping from a 1,000 foot (300m) waterfall.

SOMETIMES ILLEGAL AND ALWAYS DANGEROUS, B.A.S.E. JUMPING IS TRULY HIGH-RISK, BUT WHAT A VIEW... (LEFT TO RIGHT): BIRD'S EYE PERSPECTIVE ON THE URBAN LANDSCAPE; HURTLING IN TANDEM TOWARDS TERRA FIRMA; THE ANTENNA JUMP REQUIRES GREAT SKILL AND CONCENTRATION.

Part of the ritual of B.A.S.E. jumping is the climb to the "exit point." The process of climbing to the exit point is as much a part of B.A.S.E. jumping as the jump itself. It is during the ascent that the jumper must give careful consideration to all of the aspects of the jump they are about to make.

Visualizing the jump before it takes place allows the jumper to establish a mental image of what they are about to do, step by step. This is especially important since there simply is not enough time to think about it on the way down.

Each B.A.S.E. jump is unique. The jumper must consider all aspects of the jump prior to making it, or risk discovering an overlooked item during freefall. Only by fully considering each fall can the jumper make the most critical decision in every B.A.S.E. jump—whether or not to jump.

The ability to differentiate between a jump that can be made, and one that can but shouldn't, is probably the most important skill any B.A.S.E. jumper can possess. This is the ability to preserve one's existence based on a calculated judgment, not a simple roll of the dice, and this is what makes B.A.S.E. a sport.

Even though B.A.S.E. jumpers are extremely safety conscious, there is still a statistically high incidence of fatality. Around the world since 1981 more than 70 deaths have been recorded while B.A.S.E. jumping. These numbers only reflect those who have been killed; the number of those severely injured by non-deployment or partial deployment may be substantially higher.

I once met a B.A.S.E. jumper named Rick Harrison while with Phil Smith. Rick jumped from a building, had a partial deployment, and crushed both legs on impact. He proudly showed off his scars, and still jumps today. Given the meteoric rise in the popularity of B.A.S.E. jumping, it is fair to assume that the numbers of fatalities and injuries will increase.

For those of you who feel that B.A.S.E. jumping may be for you, be sure to find an experienced B.A.S.E. jumper or organization in your area before attempting any jumping. It is not the opinion of the author that B.A.S.E. jumping is safe, and only those with the required experience, and who are exercizing good and sober judgment, can decide if they should attempt B.A.S.E. jumping at all. For those that do, I wish you good luck.

BUNGEE JUMPING

THE IDEA OF EXPERIENCING A FREE FALL ONLY TO BE SNATCHED FROM THE JAWS OF DEATH BY A CORD ATTACHED TO THE ANKLES IS NOT NEW. BUNGEE JUMPERS CAN TRACE THE ROOTS OF THE SPORT BACK TO AN ANCIENT LEGEND TOLD BY THE NATIVE TRIBE OF PENTECOST ISLAND IN THE SOUTH PACIFIC.

Various versions of the legend exist, but the basic plot surrounds a woman who was fleeing an abusive husband. The woman climbed a tall tree and tied a vine to her ankles. Her husband followed her up and when he lunged to grab her she jumped out of the tree. He fell after her, dropping to his death while his wife was saved by the vine.

Depending on who tells the story, the men of the island started to repeat her stunt either because they were impressed by her show of courage, or just in case their wives tried the same trick. Needless to say, only men are permitted to participate in these ceremonies. The practice soon evolved into a harvest ritual.

Each year local people build a jumping tower on the side of a hill, clear the rocks away, and pulverize the dirt to soften the impact of landing. The ritual was first seen by western man when a couple of *National Geographic* writers visited the island in 1955 and reported on "land diving." It wasn't until 1970 that another *National Geographic* reporter named Kal Muller became "the first outsider known to attempt the heart-stopping plunge."

"With incredible precision (the cord) snapped taut," reported Muller. "My head barely touched dirt as I rebounded, finally coming to rest upside down... I felt oddly unshaken. The excitement had overridden any

physical discomfort." Muller's jump led to other stories about the ritual and in 1979 Oxford University's Dangerous Sportsman's Club got hold of the idea and jumped from the 245-foot (75m) Clifton Suspension Bridge in Bristol, England.

Then they brought the idea across the Atlantic, jumping from the Golden Gate Bridge in San Francisco and from a bridge spanning Colorado's Royal Gorge. With that the bungee movement in the U.S. was born.

THE MOMENT OF TRUTH, NO CHICKENING OUT. LEFT: CALIFORNIA STYLE; BELOW: ADRENALINE RUSH OVER AN OTHERWISE PEACEFUL ENGLISH VALLEY.

The early U.S. bungee jumpers were based mainly in California and spent a lot of time jumping off bridges in the Sierras. In 1987 New Zealander AJ Hackett brought a lot of attention to the sport with a jump off the Eiffel Tower. Also in 1987 the first commercial operations were started by Hackett in New Zealand and Peter and John Kockleman in the U.S., each using very different systems.

The New Zealand System uses a single, all-rubber cord that is shortened or lengthened depending on the weight of the jumper. A towel is wrapped around the ankles and the cord is attached with nylon mesh webbing. At Hackett's commercial operation, the jumper is also attached to a static safety line.

The U.S. system utilizes military-spec, nylon-wrapped shock cord and the connection is made with rock climbing harnesses and locking carabiners. Instead of lengthening or shortening the cord to accommodate weight, U.S. jumpers add or subtract shock cords. The basic formula is one cord for each 50 lbs (23kg), and each cord has a static breaking strength of 1,500 lbs (680kg), making each cord the weakest link in the system. U.S. jumpers also use two harnesses (either waist and shoulder, or custom ankle) and two anchor points for added security.

Each system has its own feel. The U.S. system is more expensive and technical. Its 2:1

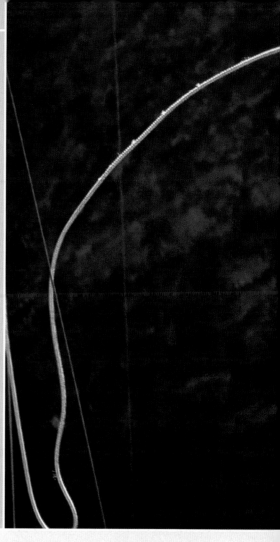

LEAP INTO OBLIVION. LEFT: ELASTIC ANKLES OVER ENGLAND; RIGHT AND FAR RIGHT: BOUNCING BACK AT KUWARA BRIDGE, QUEENSTOWN, NEW ZEALAND.

stretch ratio means more free fall and greater deceleration as the cord "catches" and begins to slow the fall. The New Zealand system has a 4:1 stretch ratio, which means that the cord is shorter and catches sooner, especially for heavier jumpers, an arrangement that is generally regarded as more comfortable.

In both systems, the energy from the jump is stored in the cords while they stretch until the fall is stopped. The stored energy then propels the jumper back upward for an additional sensation and a few subsequent free falls before the jumper comes to rest.

Bungee jumpers soon tired of simple jumps from structures and bridges and started jumping backward, by hanging from their hands or feet, or holding various positions. Others began adding novelty to bungee by jumping off in kayaks, garbage cans, riding unicycles, and other somewhat silly things.

Hardcore bungee jumpers soon began "sandbagging" to increase the intensity and height of rebound they received from the cords. Jumpers sandbag by holding onto added weight until they reach the bottom-most point of the fall, where they release the weight. This method allows a 150 lb (68kg)

jumper to be propelled upward with the stored energy of a 200 lb (91kg) jumper by releasing 50 lbs (23kg) at the bottom of the fall.

Springing back this way resulted in a whole new set of problems, since it was now possible to be propelled higher than the point from which the jumper sprang.

Jumpers took care of this by using a pendulum approach that ensured they were propelled up and away from their point of take-off. With the pendulum system, the cords are secured on the opposite side of the bridge from the jumping side. This causes the jumper to arch down into the free fall and arch up and away from the bridge on the other side.

As if sandbagging wasn't dangerous enough, jumpers began sandbagging using other jumpers as weight. The result of "the human sandbag" was a rebound that could send the jumper well above the launch point. More than a couple of jumpers have been killed or seriously injured when their partners let go too early—sometimes hundreds of feet from the ground—due to severe forces from the initial deceleration. Others have survived falls as high as 150 feet (45m). Jumpers have plunged from balloons and helicopters, seeking to add to the distance of the free fall. A handful of bungee jumpers are said to have free-fallen in excess of 1,500 feet (457m).

In an effort to increase the level of skill required to bungee jump, new approaches to bungee are being tested. Competitions that require accuracy by grasping specific targets on the ground or in the water have added a new and exciting dimension to the sport. Other more acrobatic requirements are also being integrated into bungee.

Bungee is very safe for beginners. Bungee is often considered one of the most dangerous extreme sports, when in fact it may be the safest. There have been reports of injuries to jumpers' limbs and eyes from the shock of the deceleration, however, such reports have been grossly exaggerated. In fact, statistically, it is far safer to bungee than to drive a car, and of those who have been killed or injured while bungee jumping, all events were the result of human error.

As long as the jumpers have a complete understanding of the stretch of the cords, the distance of the fall, and the weight of the jumper, the jump should be uneventful. The fact is that if all of the safety considerations are met, the cord will stop the fall just as well as brakes stop a car when traveling downhill at speed to a stop sign on a cliff.

BUNGEE JUMPING IS SAFER THAN DRIVING A CAR, IT'S JUST THAT IT DOESN'T FEEL THAT WAY. CLOCKWISE (LEFT TO RIGHT): BUNGEE JUMPING FROM A PURPOSE-BUILT TOWER; ABOVE A THRIVING METROPOLIS; BETWEEN THE SPANS OF AN ARCH.

GLIDING

GLIDING IS A RUSH ANYONE CAN EXPERIENCE. THERE IS NO NEED TO BRUISE YOURSELF LEARNING, FOR IT IS AS EASY AS FINDING A GLIDING CENTER WHERE YOU CAN RENT A RIDE.

By definition, soaring and gliding are slightly different, although they are commonly used terms to describe the sport of soaring. Soaring is defined as flying without engine power and without loss of altitude. Gliding on the other hand, is defined as flying without engine power, and a glider is an aircraft without a power source.

Gliders are towed from airfields by tow-planes using tow-ropes of between 150 and 200 feet (45 and 60m) in length. The tow-ropes are light, stretchy, abrasion-resistant lines with high strength-to-weight ratios.

Tow-ropes are designed to be dropped by the glider once the desired altitude has been achieved. The glider is then left to the task of finding ways in which to increase its altitude without assistance.

Gliders all have a "glide ratio" which refers to how many feet the craft can glide compared to the altitude that it loses in flight. So, a glide ratio of 22:1 would signify that the glider is capable of traveling 22 feet for every foot it loses in altitude.

A glide ratio of 22:1 is normal for many of today's gliders, such as the Schweizer 2-33, one of the most popular training gliders in the world. Gliders like the Schweizer have maximum speeds of around 100 mph (160kph). There are many high-performance gliders with ratios in excess of 50:1 that are capable of speeds exceeding 110 mph (176kph).

Of course once you have defined the glide ratio, you know how far your glider can fly before it reaches the ground. The object of soaring is to use rising warm air currents, or "thermals," to lift the glider at rates equal to or in excess of their glide ratio. Each time the pilot catches a thermal and rides it upward, they extend both the distance they can travel and the duration of their flight.

Understanding and being able to read the air currents in a search for thermals is where the art of soaring begins. It is also where the sport of soaring is derived. Much of soaring hinges on the pilot's ability to travel specific distances, reach predetermined locations, or pass through specific zones, maximize or minimize total time spent aloft, and a mixture of these tasks. The trick to winning is utilizing the thermals to reach your performance goals.

Reading thermals is no easy task. They are invisible, yet they can be found by reading the horizon and cloud patterns for clues to their existence. Top pilots are also sound meteorologists, who understand the meaning of cloud formations and the effects of solar radiant heating as the day progresses.

In 1964, Al Parker became the first glider pilot to fly 1,000 kilometers (621 miles) non-stop. In 1977, Karl Striedieck completed the first 1,000-mile (1,600-kilometer) non-stop glider flight.

Today, pilots continue to push the performance envelopes of their gliders. What seems to be the only barrier to the next record is technological advances in materials that can make the gliders lighter and faster with increased glide ratios.

If you're wondering who started it all, you can thank Sir George Cayley, who flew the first manned glider in 1853. Since that day, soaring and glider technology have come a long way.

Eventually the gliders were modified to be airplanes, which were modified to be tow-planes, which gliders still use today to take off and gain their initial altitude.

After WWI, the first modern soaring competition was held in Wasserkuppe, Germany in 1920. In 1921, the first soaring flight using thermals to ascend was made by Wolfgang Klemperer. The Germans went on to perfect virtually all of the important soaring equipment and techniques used today.

Soaring is certainly an exciting and challenging sport that can be enjoyed by virtually anyone seeking the thrill of powerless flight and the challenge of staying aloft using the natural forces of the wind and sun.

PERFECT PEACE. ABOVE: GLIDER AND PILOT SOAR ABOVE A MAJESTIC LANDSCAPE; RIGHT: GLIDERS AT REST; FAR RIGHT: FLOATING ABOVE RIPPLING WATER.

HANG GLIDING

HANG GLIDING IS THE CLOSEST WE CAN GET TO FLYING LIKE A BIRD. HANG GLIDING IS THE ESSENCE OF NON-MOTORIZED, UNASSISTED FLIGHT ALL OF US HAVE DREAMED OF FROM TIME TO TIME.

The sport of hang gliding continues to progress today, as new technology allows the use of lighter and stronger materials. Extreme hang gliding is found only at the top expert level, where pilots can do virtually every trick imaginable, from full barrel rolls to inverted maneuvers. Stunt flying is a rapidly growing, and dangerous facet of hang gliding.

Records in hang gliding deal with extreme distance and altitude. Distances of more than 200 miles (320km) and altitudes above 10,000 feet (3,000m) are not uncommon. In 1985, Larry Tudor set the height record of 14,250.69 feet (4,343.61m) above Horseshoe Meadows, California. In 2001, Manfred Ruhmer of Austria set the distance record of 431.14 miles (700.6km) over Zapata, Texas.

Leonardo Da Vinci too dreamt of flight, and drew many flying machines during his life. A few are remarkably similar to today's hang gliders. The first manned hang glider flown was designed, built and flown by German inventor Otto Lilienthal in 1893.

The Wright brothers are said to owe much of their success at piloting the first motorized

FREE AS A BIRD. BELOW: HANG GLIDERS WAIT THEIR TURN TO GET AIRBORNE; RIGHT: THE VIEWS ARE INCREDIBLE WHEN YOU GET YOUR OWN WINGS.

flight to their experience piloting hang gliders. However, with the emergence of power aircraft, hang gliding all but faded away into obscurity.

In the early 1960s, NASA began searching for a way to safely return the Gemini two-man orbital spacecraft to Earth. Scientists Francis and Gertrude Rogallo, at NASA's request, invented a flexible wing that would allow the spacecraft to maneuver and land without the need for a parachute.

This triangular wing design, known as the Rogallo Wing, is what led to the design of the first sport hang gliders. The Rogallo design created a foil that was easier to control, and thereby opened the sport of hang gliding up to a whole new group of enthusiasts.

Pilots launch their hang gliders from hills or cliffs from a running start to generate the initial lift necessary for flight. Once aloft, the pilot must seek rising zones of warm air called "thermals." The pilot then circles within the thermal and they are lifted up as if they were in an elevator. Strong thermals can easily lift a hang glider 3,000 feet (915m). The pilot can then seek out additional thermals for added lift, or fly around until they require a further thermal to once again get to higher altitude.

Improvements to the design of hang gliders, stemming from the Rogallo Wing and other technological advances have produced a tremendous rise in the popularity of hang gliding. Basically, these improvements have created hang gliders that are easier to fly, more comfortable, and much harder to crash.

Before some of the modern teaching techniques were developed, students had to struggle through a trial and error learning process and were forced to attempt new maneuvers cold. Flying a hang glider requires familiarizing oneself with the feel of each maneuver, which can often prove to be a long, difficult, and sometimes painful process. It is this factor that used to discourage many from pursuing the sport.

Learning to hang glide has become far easier with the introduction of tandem training techniques. Tandem training allows a qualified instructor to fly with their trainee and demonstrate new maneuvers in real-time, allowing students to get the "feel" of a move without having to master it first. It is estimated that this technique can shorten the learning curve for hang gliders by as much as 30 per cent. One of the principal reasons for the shortened curve is that tandem instruction allows beginners to experience and get the feel of even the most intricate maneuvers without the need to master hang gliding first.

Once a beginner has learned to hang glide solo, they start out flying beginner

WINGS OF OPPORTUNITY. LEFT: THE PILOT LOOKS FOR THERMALS, RISING ZONES OF WARM AIR, ON WHICH TO GAIN ALTITUDE; ABOVE: FEW THINGS ARE AS PEACEFUL AS FLOATING OVER WOOD AND HILLS.

"ships" that are much less streamlined than performance versions. These beginner models are far more forgiving, allowing for some pilot error while skills are developed.

Once they've learned the nuances of hang gliding flight, they are no longer considered to be a "wuffo," which in hang gliding circles means a bad pilot or someone who knows nothing about the sport.

Hang gliders are deceptively strong. They are built of aircraft quality aluminum and stainless steel with a sail (the wing) generally made of dacron. The structure is held together by a series of wires that create an amazingly stable geometry. A typical hang glider is capable of handling a load of over one ton without breaking. Today's hang glider technology allows them to be outfitted with full instrumentation, radios, and even rocket deployed emergency parachutes.

For readers wishing to try their hand at hang gliding, look to your local organizations which can provide you with training manuals or videos, and tell you where to get proper instruction. Everyone dreams of flying like a bird, hang gliding offers the chance to do it.

HIGH WIRE

TIGHTROPE WALKERS HAVE ALWAYS CAPTURED THE IMAGINATION OF CIRCUS CROWDS. THE DAREDEVIL PERFORMERS OFTEN WALKED WITHOUT THE AID OF A NET TO CATCH THEM SHOULD THEY FALL.

The famous Flying Walenda family of tightrope performers have achieved countless amazing high wire walks, including one which was captured live on television. Millions watched in shock as the senior Walenda fell to his death from a high wire walk between high-rise buildings, several floors above the ground.

There are very few high wire performers in the world. Of the few who practice high wire, Jay Cochrane, a 51-year-old Canadian, is the most extreme by far.

Jay holds the Guinness certified world record for the longest and highest high wire walk. He also holds the world record for time spent balancing on a high wire—21 days and nights spent performing six shows a day to the crowds in San Juan, Puerto Rico.

He set the record for height and distance when he traveled to China and crossed the Qutang Gorge on a 1⅛-inch (29mm) diameter zinc-coated steel wire. The wire was strung a distance of 2,098 feet (640m) across the gorge. The distance from the wire to the Yangtze River which formed the gorge, an incredible 1,350 feet (412m).

The Chinese government estimated that 100,000 Chinese watched in person while hundreds of millions tuned in on state-run television to witness Cochrane's feat

Jay performs all of his high wire stunts without the aid of a net. His only equipment is a 40 foot long (12m), 60 lb (27kg) titanium balancing pole, which he uses to stabilize himself as he walks. It is unlikely that this extreme sport will gain an enormous following of aspiring high wire record setters, or high wire walkers for that matter.

This sport requires split-second reflexes, and a willingness to play a life and death game with each record attempt. For those, like Jay Cochrane, it is the ultimate test, for which they are willing to pay the ultimate price.

FAR LEFT: FREDI NOCK BREAKING THE WORLD RECORD, ST MORITZ; LEFT: ZHANG SHENG LING ABOVE THE GREAT WALL OF CHINA; BELOW: JAY COCHRANE.

SKI JUMPING

FOR AS LONG AS THERE HAVE BEEN SKIS, PEOPLE HAVE SOUGHT OUT THE RUSH THAT EVEN A SMALL LAUNCH INTO THE AIR PROVIDES. AND TOP JUMPERS KEEP GOING FURTHER IN THEIR SEARCH FOR THRILLS.

In the small town of Telemark, Norway, Sondre Norheim revolutionized skiing when he developed the loose heel binding system for nordic (cross country) skiers in 1861. The "telemark" turn and style of nordic skiing was born from the techniques Sondre developed, and soon accomplished nordic skiers began building small jumps to test their skills.

The first nordic skiing and jumping contests are believed to have been held in 1892. The first dedicated jumping hill was built in Oslo in that same year. That location is still host to the annual Holmenkollen Ski Festival.

As Norwegians began emigrating to other countries, most notably the U.S. and Canada, they brought their nordic skills with them, and nordic skiing and jumping competitions gained a new base of enthusiasts.

In 1924, ski jumping was included in the first Winter Olympics. The "Nordic Combined" Olympic medals are awarded to athletes competing for best in the world honors for combined cross country racing and ski jumping ability to this day.

As ski jumping matured, many techniques were created in an effort to travel the maximum distance possible. A scoring system for jumps was created that considered not only distance but also style for each jumper. Over time, jumping styles included "windmilling" their arms while in flight, stretching their arms forward until landing, leaning over their skis in a jack-knife position, and finally the modern "V" style. Each style was considered state of the art for its time.

As ski jumping styles changed, so did the skis themselves, gradually becoming longer and wider. Modern jumping skis average 8ft 2in–8ft 10in (2.50–2.65m) in length and are roughly twice the width of traditional nordic skis. As the skis got longer and wider, they added lift to the skier, thus making for longer and longer jumps.

Olympic ski jumping hills have traditionally measured 90 and 120 meters (300 and 395 feet). The rating is based on the distance from the jump to the "K Point" on the hill. The K-Point is the point at which the hill begins its transition to a flat surface. To illustrate this measurement, a 90-meter jump has a K-Point that is 90 meters from the jump, a 120-meter jump has a K-Point that is 120 meters... and so on. As ski jumping equipment enabled jumpers to clear the K-Point by greater and greater distances, a new K-Point was needed.

THE TAKE-OFF. CLOCKWISE (FROM THE LEFT): THE CLASSIC SKI JUMP WITH TAKE-OFF POINT SLOPING DOWNWARD 11°; THE "V" STYLE, A CURRENT FAVORITE WITH JUMPERS; SLOW ASCENT AS JUMPERS CLIMB TO TAKE THEIR PLACE IN THE QUEUE.

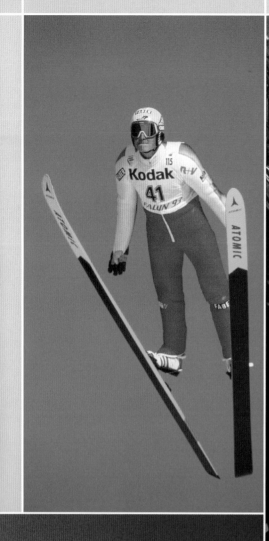

The new K-Point was established at 140 meters (460 feet), and the sport of ski jumping became the sport of ski flying. The basic techniques are the same for ski flying as ski jumping. Today, the most frequently used technique is the "V" style in which the skier points the skis so that the tails are nearly touching, and the tips are wide apart, creating a V shape.

With the "V" style, skiers are able to use the additional lift the position offers, and fly a trajectory that keeps them only 10 feet (3m) above the slope below them, while with older techniques had the skier hovering 20 or more feet above the slope. To jump, the skier starts down the hill to the jump site from a seated position high above the take-off point. Skiers crouch down to optimize their aerodynamic form and minimize wind resistance. In this position, they accelerate to speeds exceeding 60 mph (96kph) before reaching their take-off point. At the take off point, the skiers lunge forward toward the tips of their skis, adding the final lift-generating form, their body. The take-off point is not flat, but sloped downward at 11 degrees.

On landing, the skier uses a traditional telemark-style position, with one foot in front of the other. In that position, the front foot is flat with the knee bent, and the back heel is slightly elevated with the knee low and bent.

This is the correct landing position for both ski jumping and ski flying.

Each jump is scored based on the style of the jump from take-off to the landing, and the distance traveled relative to the K-Point. Style points are awarded by a panel of five judges. Each can award up to 20 points for style. The highest and lowest scores are discarded, and the sum of the remaining scores is the skier's style total. Therefore, the maximum style points available to a jumper is 60.

Distance points based on the K-Point are added or subtracted based on a predetermined scale and are given in meter and half-meter increments. Skiers reaching the K-Point are automatically awarded 60 points. Distances beyond or short of the K-Point add or subtract from the overall distance score. Distance points are added to style points, and a winner is chosen. The current distance world record is held by Andreas Goldberger, from Austria, who flew 225 meters (738ft) in 2000.

One of the less structured extreme ski jumping styles is referred to as galondee. In galondee jumping, skiers jump for distance using traditional alpine skiing equipment. Alpine skis use a fixed heel and toe binding system with rigid boots. Alpine skiing is the style generally practiced at ski resorts using lift-served terrain.

Galondee jumps are not nearly as long distance as ski jumping or flying using nordic equipment, since the fixed heel limits the skier's ability to generate lift. While galondee jumping can be done on ski jumping hills, it is often done in natural settings using steep hills with bumps and drop-offs that are available. Galondee jumping competitions do exist, however, the spirit of most events is less structured than galondee jumping's Olympic counterparts.

THE VIEWS ARE AWESOME IF YOU CAN STAY UPRIGHT. CLOCKWISE (LEFT TO RIGHT): ON TOP OF THE WORLD; THOMAS MORGENSTERN TAKES A TUMBLE IN THE K120 WORLD SKI JUMPING; SVEN HANNAWALD PREPARES FOR LIFT-OFF.

SKY DIVING

THE EXCITEMENT OF PLUMMETING TO EARTH WITH THE TIME TO THINK AND ENJOY THE VIEW IS WHAT ATTRACTS SO MANY TO JUMP FROM AIRPLANES ALONG WITH OTHERS OF A LIKE MIND.

ARTISTS OF THE FLOATING WORLD.
ABOVE: SKY DIVERS AT SUNSET OVER TITUSVILLE,
FLORIDA. RIGHT: FREE FALLERS GET TO GRIPS WITH
ONE ANOTHER OVER COCOA BEACH, FLORIDA.

Over the years, sky diving has evolved from what was once a necessary skill of self-preservation to the source of inspiration for other sports like sky surfing and B.A.S.E. jumping.

The high standards developed for both jump schools and jumping operations have made sky diving a relatively safe sport. According to the United States Parachuting Association, in 2002, there were 33 deaths from more than 2.15 million jumps by USPA members, suggesting that sky diving may well be safer than driving a car in many places.

Traditionally, sky diving students have been taught by the "static line" method which automatically deploys the jumper's chute once clear of the aircraft. This method allows for no free fall time, so most schools are moving to the tandem and accelerated free fall methods of instruction. In a tandem jump, the student can experience the thrill of free fall while safely connected to a certified instructor. The AFF method then allows the student to jump solo and free fall in the company of instructors, who free fall with the student until they successfully deploy their chute.

Another benefit of the evolution of sky diving is the development of the square "Ram Air"-style parachute which allows jumpers to steer their chutes and provides additional lift compared to the older round chutes. The additional lift makes for a softer landing, too.

Having progressed through the learning stages (generally 15-plus jumps), new sky divers are ready to try more difficult maneuvers and tests of skill. With practice, they can soon participate in the sport of sky diving, including events like accuracy contests, formation free fall, canopy stacking, canopy relative work, freestyle, and perhaps even sky surfing and B.A.S.E. jumping if they're so inclined.

Shortly before WWI, the idea of parachuting for sport was born when bi-plane tours became a popular attraction at fairs. In 1930, the first known parachuting contest was held in Russia. Contestants were scored on their ability to hit a ground target.

Target accuracy is an aspect of parachuting competition that is still practiced today. Present day targets are merely 20 inches (500mm) in diameter. The current record for accuracy is held by Russian sky diver Linger Abdurakhmanov, who landed on the target disk an incredible 50 consecutive times.

Formation free fall events take place when several sky divers free fall together, then move into positions enabling them to hold on to one

another in formation. The danger of formation free fall stems from the possibility of a high-speed collision mid-air, causing one or more jumpers to lose consciousness. The use of an Automatic Deployment Device (ADD) is one way to ensure that unconsciousness does not lead to a non-deployment. The current world record for free fall formation is held by 300 sky divers who managed to link up over Eloy, Arizona in 2002.

Another style of formation jumping occurs after deployment. In stacked canopy formation sky diving, the jumpers deploy their chutes and then physically hook their legs into the lines of the open canopy of a jumper below. Another series of jumpers then stack themselves on the canopies of the linked jumpers, until the final formation is completed.

The biggest risk in this form of formation sky diving is that the jumpers can get entangled in the canopies of other jumpers with deadly results. Jumpers all carry secondary canopies in case they must cut themselves free of entanglement. The current World Record was set in 2003 when 64 jumpers fell into a stacked canopy formation

TEAM WORK. BELOW: "RAM-AIR" PARACHUTES ALLOW LIFT AND FLEXIBILITY IN DESCENT. RIGHT: IT'S CALLED "CANOPY RELATIVE WORK" —HERE 80 WOMEN TRY FOR A NEW WORLD RECORD IN FRANCE, 1990.

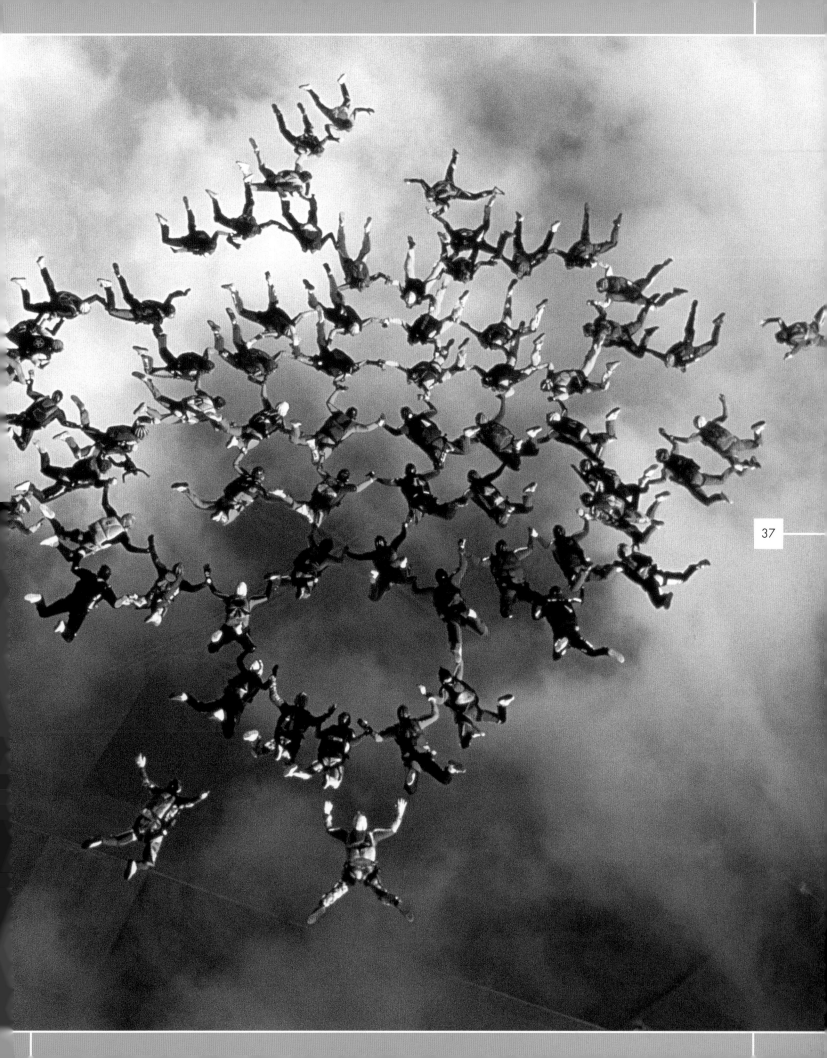

SKY DIVING IS NOTHING BUT PLANE SAILING. CLOCKWISE (FROM BOTTOM LEFT): THE REAL MILE-HIGH CLUB; THROWING CAUTION TO THE WINDS; "CANOPY RELATIVE WORK" – SKY DIVERS OVER, GARDINER, NEW YORK; SUNSET ABOVE THE CLOUDS; LEAVING A HELICOPTER BY THE EMERGENCY EXIT.

over Lake Wales, Florida. The canopy relative work (CPW) event consists of two or more sky divers working together to form geometric formations. Geometric forms are created through aerial maneuvers that are judged.

Freestyle sky diving is an aerial ballet that is captured on camera for judging. The freestyle sky diver performs an assortment of airborne gymnastic maneuvers prior to deploying their chute, and is judged on the style and artistic elements of the jump.

The sport of sky diving has an interesting history. There are reports of parachute-like devices being used in 12th century China as well as 16th century Venice. The first documented use of a parachute was in 1783, the same year balloons were first being experimented with. A large audience in Paris watched as stunt performer Andre Germain jumped with a parachute in 1797. In 1808, Jodaki Kuparento bailed out of a burning balloon several thousand feet above Warsaw in the first documented emergency use of a parachute. He survived.

Of course, most of the styles of sky diving would not be possible had Frenchman Leo Valentin not developed a technique for stabilized free fall in 1948. The fact that sky divers could free fall for prolonged periods under control is what led to the establishment of much of the modern sky diving doctrine. The first Parachuting World Championships were held shortly thereafter in 1951 in the former Yugoslavia.

The sport of sky diving is one of the easiest of the extreme sports to learn, and dive centers are located in every major region of the world. Anyone considering learning should seek out a center with new equipment and a history of quality instruction.

SKY SURFING

PARACHUTISTS HAVE LONG EXPERIMENTED WITH DIFFERENT WAYS OF STEERING THEIR BODIES THROUGH THE AIR. IT WAS SIMPLY A MATTER OF TIME BEFORE SOMEONE CAME UP WITH THE IDEA OF SKY SURFING.

First, as early as 1980, a few skydivers in California started testing free fall while lying on top of boogie boards. These pioneers found that the boards added quite a bit of speed and directional control but, most importantly, proved in principle that jumping with boards could be done.

Next, Frenchman Joel Cruciani succeeded in jumping while standing on a small surfboard which had been modified by mounting snowboard bindings to it. Joel strapped in and became the first skysurfer, a stunt that was featured in the film *Hibernator*.

This board was reportedly unstable and difficult to surf on due to the size of the surface

CATCHING A WAVE – IN COMPETITION, A SKY SURFER AND HIS CAMERA MEN ARE SCORED AS A TEAM. LEFT: THE SWEDISH SKY SURFING TEAM IN TRAINING OVER FLORIDA; RIGHT: FURTHER UP THE EASTERN SEABOARD, A SKYSURFER OVER NEW YORK STATE.

he needed to control in flight which tended to catch in the air currents and capsize.

In 1988, another French sky diver, by the name of Laurent Bouquet, began experimenting with boards for free fall. His design used a skateboard-sized board that strapped to his feet. It was obviously much smaller than Cruciani's, and very easily controlled.

In 1989, yet another Frenchman, expert B.A.S.E. jumper and extreme parachutist the late Patrick de Gayardon, designed and perfected a binding cut-away system that allowed a sky surfer to release the board should he lose control in free fall.

The addition of this binding system provided the opportunity for sky surfers to experiment with a number of shapes and sizes, evolving to the snowboard shape that is the favorite of most sky surfers. Later that year, de Gayardon portrayed the "Silver Surfer" for film-maker Thierry Donard's *Pushing the Limits 2*.

By 1990, the Silver Surfer inspired other European jumpers to try sky surfing. Soon news spread throughout the sky diving world

of this new and exciting sport, and the stage was set for its exponential growth over the next six years. Many new tricks evolved as the sky surfers pushed the limits of their sport.

In the fall of 1990. the World Freestyle Federation (WFF) staged the first World Freestyle Championships in Texas, and introduced sky surfing as a featured demonstration. The 1990 World Freestyle Championships marked the first time that the "team video concept" was used.

WFF founder Pete Mckeeman was the first to envision using a "camera-flyer" to capture a sky surfer's performance for judging purposes. Sky surfing instantly became a made-for-TV sport, accelerating the already rapid growth.

The introduction of a free-falling, cameraman partner into sky surfing created an entirely new series of complications. The highly maneuverable sky surfer is capable of traveling at speeds that can exceed 120 mph (193kph) in many directions during free fall. The cameraman also travels downward at similar speeds. Should the two collide the result can be unconsciousness or worse.

Therefore, sky surfers and their cameraman partners use an AAD, or Auto Activation Device. The auto-deployment takes place at a predetermined altitude or time to prevent non-deployment in the case of injury

or loss of consciousness. Sky surfers also run the risk of spinning out of control, in which case the AAD also proves invaluable.

In competition, a sky surfer and cameraman are scored as a team. With team video scoring, it is the overall presentation that is judged. How the camera-flyer positions himself during free fall, how he frames his shots, and how in-synch he can stay with the sky surfer all factor into the score.

The resulting footage and the sport itself have evolved into a highly synchronized free fall ballet—with the sky surfer and camera-flyer executing simultaneous rolls, flips, and spins while hurtling toward the ground at around 120 mph.

Winning teams display a coherence and consistency of movement between the sky surfer and the cameraman that is uncanny. At larger competitions, a direct feed from the camera-flyer's camera to a "jumbotron" monitor on the ground allows spectators to see the performance in real-time.

Sky surfing is very exciting to watch. For those wishing to try their hand at it, this is a sport to be left to only the very best and most experienced sky divers. For example, two time Sky Surfing World Champion Joe Jennings was killed in 1996 while sky surfing for a commercial in California, reportedly victim to a partial deployment.

SKY FLYING

THE FUTURE OF EXTREME SPORTS LIES IN REFINING EXISTING SPORTS. KITE BOARDING HAS DRAGGED WINDSURFERS INTO THE TWENTY-FIRST CENTURY, AND SKY FLYING COULD DO THE SAME FOR SKY DIVING.

In the same way that using a jet ski to get into waves in the 50ft range has taken surfing to a new level, Felix Baumgartner's idea—to develop an aerodynamic wing suit and strap a carbon wing to his back in a bid to control freefall—has thrown the world of sky diving into turmoil. This is how one man's vision could change the way we look at the skies.

Sky diving is a sport that is accustomed to change. Over the last 20 years sky divers have been experimenting with different ways to enhance the sensation of freefall, the feeling of experiencing the maximum freedom with the mimimum possible genuine danger.

Probably the most successful and high-profile sibling of sky diving is B.A.S.E. jumping. The idea behind B.A.S.E. jumping was to bring the ground closer to increase the fear. A truly extreme measure that has created easily the most dangerous sport on earth, where one in seven participants will suffer severe injury or death in their jumping career.

Sky surfing first took to the skies in the early Eighties when sky divers started strapping snowboards, surfboards and skateboards to their feet and took them with them up into the clouds in a bid to become real-life

THE RIGHT STUFF. LEFT AND BELOW: FELIX BAUMGARTNER IN FLIGHT OVER THE ENGLISH CHANNEL; HURTLING THROUGH THE SKY.

versions of the Silver Surfer.

Despite these innovations it took until 2000 for the concept of flying to reach sky diving. The genesis for the idea belongs, fittingly to one of the most decorated B.A.S.E. jumpers in the world, Felix Baumgartner.

In 1999 Baumgartner achieved legendary status after B.A.S.E. jumping from both the statue of Christ in Rio de Janeiro and the Petronas Towers in Kuala Lumpur—the tallest manmade structures in the world.

Having reached the peak of B.A.S.E. jumping he turned his attention back to sky diving in 2000.

The idea of flying is something that has occupied the minds of sci fi enthusiasts for centuries, but Baumgartner, a mechanic by trade was sure that he could make it a reality. He started with an aerodynamic wing suit that would allow him to glide.

Early footage of this suit being tested shows Felix literally sky diving down steep mountains, while gliding across the faces of the steep slopes.

These early, and quite frankly, terrifying steps would go on to bear fruit in the shape of a small gliding wing that would attach to Felix's back and allow him to glide.

The first prototype took the form of a carbon fibre wing designed by Rudiger Kunz, the world's leading aerodynamics expert. It

was constructed by a company specializing in carbon construction for Formula One. Eventually, after extensive testing that saw Felix strapped to the top of a Porsche 911 car to test the wing at speeds of around the 200mph (320kph) mark, he announced that he would be attempting to fly across the English Channel.

The Channel measures some 22 miles (35km) across and is one of the world's busiest shipping highways. Despite being dropped off at over 30,000 feet (9,000m), higher than Everest, he would have to travel 21 feet (6m) across for every three feet (one meter) he dropped if his crossing was to be successful.

On 31 July 2003, Felix Baumgartner succeeded in his quest to cross the English Channel with room to spare and, in the process, completely opened up the world of unpowered human flight. He braved temperatures in the region of –40°C and traveled at speeds upward of 225 mph (360kph). In short he has moved into a realm of extreme sports that will take decades to explore to its full potential. The main reason for this is that, due to the constraints of funding, research and development, and of course air traffic control restrictions, it is incredibly difficult to secure actual flight time. On top of this, there is a debate between purist sky divers and Felix about the use of such a wing.

Either way one thing is certain, the history of extreme sports is living proof that progress cannot be halted. In the next 20 years there is a very real possibility that we will be out on a summer's day watching human aerobatics shows as people fly around with wings on their backs. Don't believe me? Did you think someone would be able to skyfly across the English Channel back in 2002?

HOMECOMING HERO. BELOW: THE HUMAN ROCKET IS BACK ON TERRA FIRMA; RIGHT: FELIX BAUMGARTNER IS ALONE WITH THE ELEMENTS AT 30,000 FEET (9,000M) OVER THE ENGLISH CHANNEL DURING HIS WORLD RECORD FLIGHT IN 2003

LAND SPORTS

THERE ARE MANY NATURAL ELEMENTS WE REFER TO AS LAND THAT CAN BE EXTREME AND PARTICULARLY CHALLENGING FOR SURVIVAL, NEVERMIND THE PURSUIT OF SPORT.

Consider the deserts, mountains, and glaciers that cover much of our planet. These landscapes have secured borders and civilizations over the centuries.

A would-be conqueror whose forces lacked desert survival or mountaineering skills would be ill advised to try to beat the elements and his enemy at the same time. Recent history, when the massed forces of the former Soviet Union invaded Afghanistan or U.S. forces came to grief in Somalia, shows that an understanding of survival skills and terrain can sometimes resist even a high-tech invader.

We are fortunate that extreme sports are not about conquering others, only the limitations of the athlete's mind, body, and equipment. Most land-based extreme sports take place in areas that would have hardly been considered hospitable a century ago. Thanks to technology, we can now travel to, and play in, these places in relative comfort.

However, technology has not been able to change the landscape of the harshest elements, or replace the skill sets necessary to survive in them.

Technology and change have created some new landscapes nonetheless. The urban elements are the endless miles of pavement, the stairs made from cement and stone and the railings affixed to them.

As with the natural elements, the urban elements bring with them a new set of challenges and opportunities for sport. The urbanscape is also more accessible than natural elements. As a result, urban extreme sports are the ones most likely to satisfy athletes who can't play in the natural elements due to either time or money.

It was the existence of each of these elements that spawned each extreme sport, not the harshness of the landscapes or the number of man-made obstacles that have been

THE CHALLENGES OF DIFFERENT TERRAINS. CLOCKWISE (FROM NEAR RIGHT): SKATEBOARDING IN SALVADOR, MEXICO; SCALING A SHEER ROCKFACE; EXTREME SKIING IN NEW ZEALAND; CAVING.

created. It was, to paraphrase legendary explorer and mountaineer Sir Edmund Hillary, "because they were there."

This was more than just a witty statement. In this phrase is the soul and the spirit of extreme pursuit. Hillary did not ascend Mount Everest because he needed to for survival. He did so to push his personal limits physically and mentally.

Extreme athletes look at the landscape differently than "normal" people. Climbers traveling through mountainous regions look at the series of potential routes on each face as they pass by. "Normal" folk simply see nice mountains. Skateboarders and inline skaters walk through a city park and see the flora and fauna, but tend to focus on the curbs, stairs, and railings as personal challenges to their technical abilities.

"Normal" folks walk through parks and see only the birds and squirrels.

Land-based extreme sports have the greatest diversity of terrain. Each sport requires the athlete to be able to ascend, descend, jump, and coast through any number of circumstances and unexpected obstacles. Quick reflexes and absolute focus quickly separate the best from the simply good.

It is difficult to envision what the next extreme sport to be born will be as we redraw our urban landscapes and develop new materials that will allow us to redefine performance and perhaps better survive the harsher elements.

As man and technology change and improve, our ability to test ourselves within our natural and urban environments will change. Extreme athletes seeking to push their limits will adapt new technology and thinking, creating new opportunities for future extreme athletes to redefine how to have fun on the planet.

GETTING AROUND ON WHEELS. CLOCKWISE (FROM BOTTOM LEFT): LANDSAILING AT SUNSET; EXTREME INLINE SKATING; FREERIDING ON A SNOWBOARD; GETTING SOME AIR ON A BMX; MOUNTAIN BIKING.

ACW CLIMBING

INDOOR CLIMBING FACILITIES HAVE BROUGHT WITH THEM THE ARTIFICIAL CLIMBING WALL. BECAUSE OF THEIR EASY ACCESS IN URBAN AREAS, ACWS HAVE BECOME A MAJOR DRAW AT GYMS.

ACWs have enabled an entire group of athletes, who may not have ever been exposed to climbing, to get a taste and, if hooked, to learn substantial skill sets before ever venturing out to a real rock face.

The same skills of balance, stance, and movement needed on rock and ice (crampon and ice axe use excluded) are required to climb walls, and with the many new materials and modular construction techniques, ACWs can recreate any level of climb desired, except for constraints on the height of the climb that natural settings don't have. ACWs aid both experienced climbers and those new to the sport to achieve the flexibility, finesse, and strength required as well as allowing them to maintain the commitment to the sport that top climbers must have to be successful.

Climbing competitions are judged on the basis of a climber's ability to get through difficult routes without falling, and the speed at which the climber is able to ascend the wall. There are categories for both speed and difficulty in most competitions. International climbing competitions on ACWs have been organized since 1987 when the former Soviet Union began holding speed climbing events. The first World Championships were held in 1991 in Frankfurt, Germany, allowing the International Olympic Committee to offer the sport Olympic status that same year.

The difficulty of competitions is judged by determining the highest point on the route each competitor reaches within a set period of time. Each climber must climb the route "on-sight," without seeing the route before their climb, and without witnessing others attempting it. Speed events are held on easier routes and are normally held in a double-elimination-style format, with two climbers racing simultaneously. The first to complete the route wins that heat. Losing two heats eliminates a climber.

CLOCKWISE (FROM NEAR RIGHT): GETTING TO GRIPS WITH AN ACW: WORLD SPEED CLIMBING CHAMPIONSHIPS, BIRMINGHAM, ENGLAND; BETWEEN A ROCK AND A HARD PLACE: ROCK AND ICE.

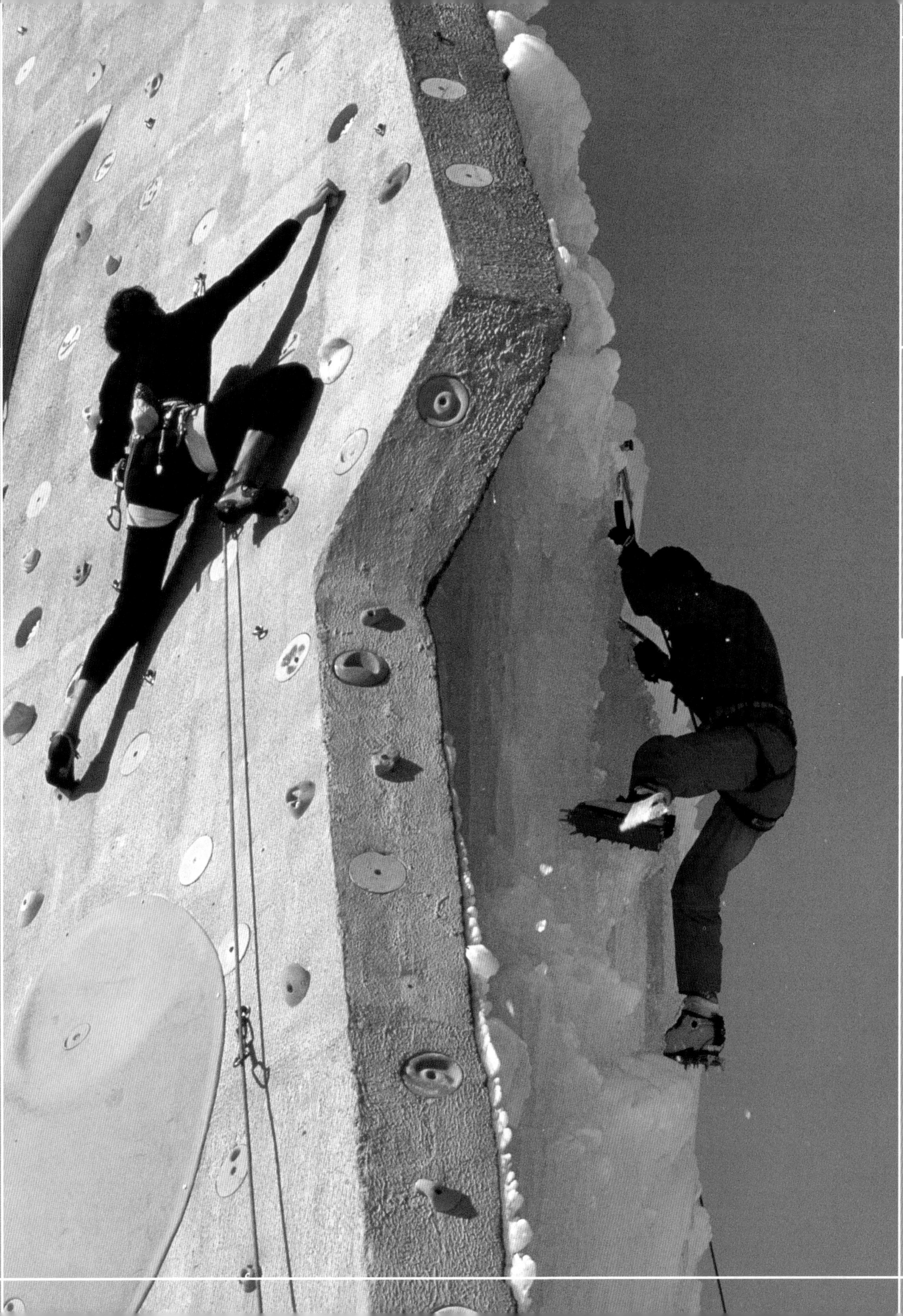

ADVENTURE RACING

MANY WOULD ARGUE THAT TRIATHLONS ARE THE MOST GRUELING TESTS OF AN ATHLETE'S PHYSICAL CONDITIONING AND MENTAL TOUGHNESS. THE IRONMAN IS AN EVENT THAT DRAWS THE WORLD'S TOP TRIATHLETES FROM 75 COUNTRIES TO HAWAII EACH YEAR IN OCTOBER.

What makes the Ironman the most extreme triathlon is not its distance—many world class triathlons have similar distances—but the weather. Temperatures, with highs averaging 88°F (31°C) and humidity levels between 40 and 85 per cent, are sometimes accompanied by 60 mph (97kph) winds. Athletes can expect to endure conditions that make this one event more torturous than most.

The Ironman got its start in 1978, when Navy Commander John Collins created a race based on three existing races: The Waikiki Rough Water Swim of 2.4 miles (3.9km), the Around Oahu Bike Race of 112 miles (180 km), and the Honolulu Marathon of 26.2 miles

(42.2km). The first Ironman took place on Kialua, but was moved after three years to Kona to avoid the traffic around Honolulu.

Another race that can hardly be deemed anything less than extreme is the Raid Gauloises, an event that got its start as a ten-day, 400-mile (644km) stage race conceived by French journalist Gérard Fusil. The race takes place in a different area of extreme outback each year, such as Madagascar, Borneo, and Patagonia.

The Raid Gauloises participants are five-person teams from various countries sponsored by a variety of corporations. The teams race up and down 14,000-foot

(4,267m) mountains, through swamps and down rivers, taking a massive toll on the team members, both physically and mentally. Each team member must complete the race for their team to be scored as finished. The Raid is a survivalist's dream race, arguably calling on more mental toughness than any other race in the world. This is clearly not a weekend warriors endeavor.

The Raid Gauloises has given birth to a

TRIANGULAR COMPETITION. CLOCKWISE (FROM TOP LEFT): BIKES AWAIT CONTESTANTS AT QUEENSTOWN, NEW ZEALAND, BEFORE THE ITU WORLD TRIATHLON; THE BIG SWIM, NICE, 1986; TAKING GIANT STRIDES.

53

new adventure racing trend, with several aspiring adventure races establishing themselves, including the Eco-Challenge Series promoted by Survivor producer Englishman Mark Burnett, a former Raid participant. The Eco-Challenge has established itself as the foremost adventure race in the world, attracting a wide range of participants as well as global television coverage.

Adventure racing in many ways appears to be a response to life in a world largely protected from threats to survival and the necessity of pioneering new frontiers.

It is easy to draw parallels between what these teams are doing for sport and what mankind has done for centuries to redefine our borders. The major difference today is that should we run into a life-threatening problem during one of these events, a heli-lift to safety is not far off.

In fact, most adventure races now employ the use of hand-held GPS (Global Positioning Satellite) systems that not only enable the competitors to establish where they are within a few meters, but also enable rescuers to find them quickly if need be. There are devices called sextants, once used to navigate the seas and land by reading the stars, but they can be rendered useless by clouds, and can only be read by those holding them, and not those seeking to offer rescue.

Adventure racing draws from many different extreme sports: climbing, whitewater, and mountain biking for example.

Surely event organizers and creators will find ways of including more and more extreme sports in their events until a decathlon style event is created which will act to find the best all-around extreme sports athlete in the world.

CLOCKWISE (FROM THE LEFT): ROPED TOGETHER FOR THE RAID GAULOISES, ARGENTINA, 1995; THE SYDNEY HARBOUR SWIM CLASSIC, MARCH 2003; NAVIGATING A SEA OF TWIGS AND LOGS IN THE RAID GAULOISES, BORNEO, 1994; WHITEWATER ACTION, RAID GAULOISES, BORNEO, 1994.

AGGRESSIVE INLINE SKATING

THE GROUND BROKEN BY SKATEBOARDERS OVER THE PAST THREE DECADES HAS BEEN INVADED BY AGGRESSIVE INLINE SKATERS WHO HAVE CO-OPTED MUCH OF THEIR STYLE AND CULTURE.

Inline skates can trace their roots back to the Chicago Skate Company, and perhaps further, as evidence of wheeled boots dates back to the early days of bicycling. But it wasn't until brothers Scott and Brennan Olsen created the first Rollerblades in their Minneapolis basement in 1979, that the sport took off.

The brothers stumbled on a pair of Chicago Skate Company's inline skates in the bargain bin of a used equipment store while looking for a way to train for hockey in the off season. The skates offered minimal support and awful wheels. The Olsens added greater support and urethane wheels, and the rest is history.

Scott Olsen bought the patent for inline skates from the Chicago Skate Company and began the Rollerblade Company. The first Rollerblades were nothing more than hockey boots with an inline chassis. By 1983, Scott Olsen sold Rollerblade to Robert Nagle, Jr. With new capital resources, new and improved Rollerblades were developed, and the beginning of a growth curve unparalleled in the sporting goods industry had begun.

At first, the Rollerblade inline skates were designed to provide cross-training for hockey skaters. Then skiers discovered that Rollerblades offered the ability to get a carved-turn sensation on pavement, and

became the second major group to use inline skates for cross-training. Inline skates soon became a heavily promoted and endorsed method for training in the off season within the ski industry. The third and largest group to embrace the Rollerblade phenomenon was the Eighties aerobic and fitness crowd. Fitness fanatics quickly recognized that skating was a great way to tone the legs and buttocks while increasing aerobic capacity with far lower

FITNESS AND TRAINING DEVICES HAVE BEEN TRANSFORMED INTO A NEW AREA OF SPORT. ABOVE: CHECKING OUT THE AIR DOWN BY THE SEASIDE; RIGHT: ALWAYS WEAR THE RIGHT GEAR.

impact than running. By 1989, over three million inline skates were being sold each year. By 1997, the U.S. National Sporting Goods Association estimated there were 26.6 million inline skaters in the U.S. alone.

Soon the boom in inline skating reciprocated in reported injuries from falls. Most common were broken wrists, arms, and head injuries. This prompted an aggressive effort to teach skaters to protect themselves properly by wearing wrist, elbow, knee, and head protection when skating. Use of these items has greatly reduced the risks of injury in a fall. Smart skaters, whether skating for fitness or trick skating, have all found these items work well when needed.

Naturally, it was only a matter of time before the top inline skaters would seek to redefine their sport. No longer content to skate about town in a "civilized" manner, top skaters began to search for a new, less aerobic and fitness-oriented identity. The new breed of aggressive skaters turned to the skateboard world for guidance, not only for cultural grounding but for a direction to push their sport forward. In turn, this gave way to "street style" and "vert" inline skating.

Like skateboarding, "street" inline skaters seek to jump over and grind across just about any obstacle imaginable. To do so requires special grind plates attached to the chassis of the skates, so that the wheels don't grab at inappropriate times, and the skate's chassis aren't destroyed by the moves. These needs wound up giving birth to an entire sub-industry created to serve the needs of aggressive skaters that the corporate manufactures are only now recognizing represent the future of inline skating. Open an aggressive inline magazine like *Box* or *Daily Bread* and you'll find everything from over-sized pads to T-shirts

CLOCKWISE (FROM THE LEFT): VERT SKATING TAKES ITS TERMS FROM SKATEBOARDING AS WELL AS SHARING ITS VENUES; INLINE SKATING TURNS EVERY NEIGHBORHOOD INTO A PLACE OF ADVENTURE; SKATER TAKES THE QUICK WAY DOWN.

CLOCKWISE (FROM NEAR RIGHT): KNEESY DOES IT IN THE RAIL GRIND; MASTERING THE HALF-PIPE; FABIOLA DA SILVA GOES THROUGH HIS PACES AT DISNEY'S CALIFORNIA ADVENTURE "X GAMES EXPERIENCE"; STANLEY CHOU AND STRINGER IN KUALA LUMPUR.

to Titanium skate chassis. Grind plates, custom chassis, and specialized wheels and many of the items that aggressive skaters used to fashion for themselves are now available via mail order.

Vert skating began when inliners first invaded the sacred territory of skateboarders, the half-pipe. At first, this invasion created tension at the skate parks, which in most places has died down as inliners have gotten better and now demand some respect for their abilities. Inline vert skating does differ in some ways from skateboarding vert, since the skater's feet are free to move independently. The skater who has had the most impact on technical independent foot moves presently is Australia's Matt Salerno.

His abilities are redefining vert skating, creating maneuvers that are truly the property of the aggressive inline movement.

Aggressive inline skaters have created a number of terms to define the moves they make, both on the street and when skating vert.

ABEC is an acronym for Annular Bearing Engineering Council. ABEC ratings correspond to the speed and efficiency of the bearing sets which can be replaced, removed, cleaned, and reinserted into the wheel sets. The higher the rating (between 1–5) the faster the bearing will roll.

The durometer figure is how wheels are gauged for hardness. The higher the durometer number, the harder the wheel.

Rockering is the process of lowering or raising the middle two wheels or outside two wheels to create either a flat or curved skate contact with the surface being ridden. A curved rocker allows for quicker turning while a flatter rocker allows for greater stability, especially at speed.

Spacers are small round tubes that are used to separate the bearings in each wheel and create a protective barrier between the bearing and the axle.

Chassis refers to the plastic, metal, or composite frame that is secured to the bottom of each boot and which holds the wheel sets. Designs can vary greatly. If you wear the best gear to look the part but can't skate to save your life, you'll be referred to as a "poser."

Cheese Grater Asphalt is poor or rough road conditions or surfaces.

Bail To Fall is an intentional fall to avoid a nastier wipe out.

And Slam Tan refers to tan lines caused by wearing the protective elbow, wrist, and knee protection.

BMX

JUST ABOUT EVERYONE HAS ATTEMPTED TO JUMP THEIR BIKE OVER SOMETHING WHILE GROWING UP. BMX BIKES REDEFINED WHAT COULD BE DONE, AND THE IDEA OF DIRT RACING AND STUNTS EVOLVED.

We sometimes take for granted the fact that we were influenced to try these things in the first place, and that our bikes would stand up to that kind of punishment.

But it wasn't until the small cruiser-style bikes of the Sixties and Seventies arrived that people began to change how they looked at riding a bike. Kids found that they were quite maneuverable, and the smaller wheels and fatter rubber tires made them more capable of enduring the thrashing a hard-riding kid could deliver. These new bikes opened up new terrain and with that came a hoard of new possibilities—soon kids jumping things found they could jump bigger things, and could ride on softer surfaces, and slowly the idea of dirt racing and jumping evolved naturally.

Bicycle motocross was born in Southern California in the Seventies when organizers first began setting up weekend races on special dirt tracks resembling miniature motocross circuits. The appeal of being able to motocross on your own bike was too great a temptation for millions of kids and, during the late Seventies and early Eighties, BMX became the fastest-growing youth sport in the world. But just like the first two boom/bust cultures of skateboarding, the BMX bubble burst.

It was hit even harder than skateboarding though for two reasons. Firstly, not only was it a craze, but it was succeeded by another

supposed fad, mountain biking. Mountain biking established itself as a much more sociable and practical way of using your bike and this won the hearts and minds of parents (the people buying bikes) and the BMX industry folded. This is the reason that, from the early Eighties through to the early Nineties, it was at times impossible to get BMX bikes outside America, even California, at times.

This unfortunate history is compounded by the fact that BMX was never rediscovered. It languished in obscurity for over a decade where people who remained passionate about the sport pushed their own personal boundaries and built a small but thriving industry. Without corporate involvement in the sport BMXers found it was much easier to control the destiny and progression of their chosen sport, as skateboarders had discovered to their gain in the early Nineties after the boom of the late Eighties.

Without the benefit of organized governing bodies and with only dilapidated racetracks, BMX racing all but died out. It was skateboarding that came to the rescue in the end. Becuase of the boom of the late Eighties

THE TOP RIDERS ARE HIGHLY PAID PROS, USUALLY IN THEIR EARLY TO LATE TWENTIES. LEFT: VERTICAL TAKE-OFF IN PERFECT CONDITIONS; BELOW: RIDER PARTS COMPANY WITH HIS BIKE IN MELBOURNE, AUSTRALIA.

TAKING THINGS FURTHER. CLOCKWISE (FROM NEAR RIGHT): ROOFTOP RIDE; IN THE EIGHTIES VERT RIDING IN A HALF-PIPE BECAME THE CUTTING EDGE OF BMX; SUPERMAN GOES FOR A RIDE.

the construction of skate parks and ramps was on the up again.

BMX is one of the most mentally challenging extreme sports in the world. Before anything is learnt or even attempted a rider has to come to terms with the fact that there is a polished piece of chrome between their legs waiting to puncture their body at the first sign of a slam. When you consider these consequences, it gives you some understanding of the commitment that BMXers bring to their sport. It is this heart that has bought BMX back to the forefront of the extreme sports forum.

Although today's superstars of vert, street and dirt have phenomenal skills that have propelled BMX into the twenty-first century, it is fair to say that a lot of what BMX is today is down to one man: Matt Hoffman.

While there were hundreds of pioneers at different points in BMX history, Matt Hoffman stands out as the man who has done the most as a pioneer and ambassador, both on and off his bike, since he started riding in 1984. In that time, Hoffman has all but killed himself (he actually flatlined after a concussion), as well as breaking over a hundred bones along with numerous world records.

At one stage, unhappy with the rate of his progression, Hoffman decided that it was time to up the ante again and simply removed the brakes from his bike!

He single-handedly pioneered the art of vert BMX (riding a halfpipe where the transitions go all the way to a vertical plane) and inspired a new generation of riders.

His exploration of vert riding laid the foundations for, and inspired, riders like Dave Mirra, Jamie Bestwick, Simon Tabron and Zach Shaw to create tricks like the flare, a backflip 180 degree rotation, the first 900 degree spin and the backflip tailwhip, a back flip where the frame of the bike does a 360 underneath the rider. Without Hoffman, BMX would have taken a lot longer to reach the enviable position it is in today.

As racing died off, it left groups of riders who had honed their skills on the track with no outlet for their talents. Using their own initiative riders started to build their own dirt trails in the woods or on wasteland. Perfectly sculpted tracks can be found hidden in the woods or on private land, lovingly crafted from soil that has just the right amount of clay in it. Trails are made up of a row of jumps that can be anything from three to 23 in number.

Each jump is made out of two pyramid-like constructions, one for take-off and one for landing, creating a gap in between that has to

be cleared. Trails have been a constant part of BMX's development over the last 20 years, nurturing small scenes of intense talent in many places where they are built.

There is a strict unwritten code regarding trails: if you do happen to come cross one, then you must either ask permission to ride them from someone who has built them or wait to be invited. In some cases, people are very protective and refuse to let anyone who did not help build the trails ride them. But in general, if you show respect, do not litter and repair any damage that you cause, then you shouldn't have a problem.

Flatland riding resembles a kind of pavement ballet, where riders stand and step over and around their bike frames while the bike is moving. Usually this is done on one wheel and in a circular axis so that balance can be maintained with the centrifugal force. Foot pegs are added to the front and rear axles of the bike as footholds for riders. The addition of foot pegs allows riders to spin their bikes around beneath them, and even hold the bike vertically as they ride on one wheel!

Vert and street riders also use pegs, they are used to do tricks on the half-pipe's coping, a 2.5-inch (63.5mm) diameter metal tube that sits on the top edge of every half-pipe. Street riders have used pegs to follow skateboarders in to the domain of hand rails and ledges.

The most recent progression of BMX has been on the street. BMX thrived in the realm of dirt trails, skate parks and vert ramps, but with the heavy influence of skateboarding, the closure of certain parks to BMXers and the necessity to ride being the driving force, BMXers hit the streets. The progression of bike control, tricks and riders in general has been incredible over the last five years and it has been a major factor in BMX's surge in popularity. Huge gaps, hand rails, wall rides, trees, in fact any part of the natural urban environment, are used to create new lines and combinations of tricks. The bottom line for BMX is that it has been ignored by the mainstream for so long that at its heart there now is the pure desire to ride for the love of the sport alone.

For this reason BMX will maintain its innovative status, and thick seam of creative talent, because progression is the only thing that can satisfy passion like this. There is also the added advantage that so many children try out BMX when they ride a bike. And the golden rule for all freesports is that fresh blood, new perspectives and young talent are what keep the sports progressing. In terms of the future, BMX is a very rich sport.

CLOCKWISE (FROM TOP LEFT): TOTALLY FLIPPED;
JAMES NEEDHAM AT CLAPHAM COMMON, LONDON;
ACTION FROM THE PLAYSTATION SKATEPARK,
LONDON; MIKE MULLEN LEAVES THE EARTH BEHIND.

CAVING

WALKING, SCRAMBLING ON ALL FOURS, AND CRAWLING ON YOUR BELLY INTO THE MOIST DARKNESS OF A CAVE IS NOT EVERYONE'S IDEA OF A GOOD TIME, BUT YOU CAN'T DENY THAT IT IS EXTREME.

Appropriately, those who do cave (serious cavers do not refer to their sport as spelunking or potholing) travel to the inner depths of the earth in groups of two or more. Not surprisingly, cavers are subject to many dangers that one would expect could occur in a cave, such as death by starvation, falling, asphyxiation, drowning, and hypothermia from exposure.

Cavers navigate the subterranean routes with the use of lamps on their helmets. The lamps are either carbide-style, fueled by a jet of acetylene gas like in the old days of coal mining, or newer electric lighting systems using bulbs, batteries, and intermittent-pulsing lamp technologies. Having lights is so critical to a caver's survival that, as a rule, each caver should carry at least three independent sources of light with them before entering any cave. Other equipment required for caving expeditions includes a helmet, kneepads, a small pack, good boots, gloves, and mental clarity, for a lack mental toughness can be as much to blame for caving accidents as fate.

Expert cavers can explore regions that require additional equipment such as wetsuits,

JOURNEY TO THE CENTER OF THE EARTH. BELOW: CAVERS TRAVEL TO THE INNER DEPTHS IN GROUPS OF TWO OR MORE; RIGHT: LIGHTING IS THE FIRST ESSENTIAL WHEN YOU GO DOWN INTO DARKNESS.

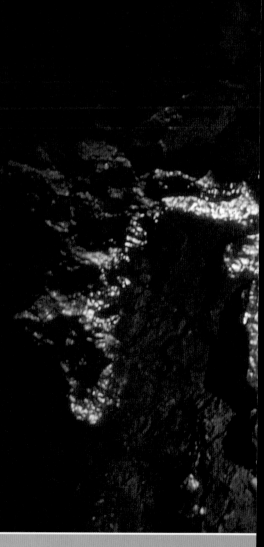

rope, climbing gear for technical sections— chocks and harnesses for ascending and rapelling—cable ladders, and scuba equipment.

All cavers and aspiring cavers can reach the point at which they can explore truly extreme terrain, however, in order to get to that point, it is recommended you join a grotto, a regional organization made up of cavers. Grottos are generally very helpful, and welcome new members and beginners as a way to grow their sport. Cavers are generally as interested in the historical and geological make up of caves they trek as they are the thrill of traveling down into the damp darkness.

Once inside, caving requires most of the same technical skill that outdoor climbers use in the daylight. Some subterranean caverns are so extensive that they dwarf many frequently climbed outdoor climbing sites.

Caving is practiced globally, especially in regions that were once under water, and so have the remains of aquatic creatures embedded in the earth which over geological time have turned to limestone. Most limestone is between 300 and 500 million years of age.

Caves offer tremendous historical evidence in some regions of the world. In France, for example, the famous Lascaux Caves have preserved drawings of prehistoric life, which now offer further insights into the origins of the human species.

Similar evidence of man's history has been discovered in caves throughout the world. One of the main reasons caves offer so much evidence of history is that they provided shelter from enemies and storage for food and property that surface structures could not. Over the centuries, caves have also been useful places to stash loot and modern treasure hunters are still hard at work seeking to find the plunder.

Caves, like the rest of the earth's treasures, are a limited and valuable resource, and a unique aspect of the global environment. There is a moral responsibility that all cavers protect the caves they explore, minimizing the gradual deterioration that occurs once a cave is discovered.

One of caving's golden rules is that cavers take out of the cave everything that they bring in, since litter and pollution have already destroyed scientifically important caves across the globe. Even accidental damage can occur that prevents cave scientists from reconstructing evidence to get a better read on our history. As a result enthusiasts are now prohibited in many places from enjoying the natural beauty of the underground world.

RIGHT: CAVING REQUIRES SIMILAR EQUIPMENT TO THAT USED IN MOUNTAINEERING; FAR RIGHT: IT IS ESSENTIAL THAT CAVERS TAKE OUT EVERYTHING THEY BRING INTO A CAVE—PROTECT THE ENVIRONMENT.

71

EXTREME MOTOCROSS

AS OFF-ROAD MOTORCYCLE RIDERS HAVE BECOME MORE SKILLED, AND AS THE EQUIPMENT AVAILABLE HAS BECOME LIGHTER AND MORE POWERFUL WITH AN EVER-INCREASING RANGE OF SUSPENSION TRAVEL, THE PHYSICAL BOUNDARIES OF WHAT CAN BE DONE ON A MOTOCROSS (MOTOX) BIKE ARE EXPANDING.

In the early days of off-road motorcycling, the thought that riders would someday leap 40 or 50 feet (12–15m) in the air, regularly, would have seemed absurd. However that is precisely the state of extreme motoX today.

Extreme riding is not as new as today's riders might make it seem, though. Hill climbs, trials riding—riders negotiate through a broad range of obstacles, requiring low speed, highly technical, balanced handling—and motoX racing have been part of motorcycle sport for years. In their day, many other riders pushed the limits of what had been done to that date. Daredevil rider Evel Knievel is a classic example of an early extreme pioneer,

who also had a better than average grasp of self-promotion.

The unique nature of the extreme sports movement today is that extreme athletes have lots of other new sports and experiences to draw on. Extreme motoX is defined by more than just racing, although race series like the AMA Supercross Series have done much to showcase the talents of top extreme riders in the world. Extreme motoX riders push their machines in ways that are new and innovative and are drawing inspiration from other sports, such as skiing and snowboarding. Many of the top riders came from the ranks of BMX riders, and so a new freestyle orientation as to how

a motoX bike is handled in the air is evident.

AMA Supercross superstar Jeremy McGrath's rise through the motoX ranks is one example of taking BMX moves and bringing them to motoX. He is also a perfect example of what can be done when skill is coupled with newer technology and lighter motoX bikes. Along with others like Jeff Emig and Kevin Windham, he is redefining what can be done on a motoX bike. The Supercross riders are also impacting how the rest of the world views motoX. The brash and unique style of the AMA pros has been backed up by their ability to win races across the globe.

The best example of extreme motoX is the

AMA Supercross Series. Here, the courses are designed to reward riders who can handle the most difficult of situations. The courses have many of the bumps and ruts of traditional motoX, but the obstacles and jumps are designed to maximize the height a rider can, and must, jump to win. Here is a brief description of a typical Supercross layout.

The start—as in traditional forms of motoX racing, the riders line up behind "the gate," a series of aluminum tubes that fall away from the riders when the start occurs. From here the riders go into start straight, where they tear out of the start and are forced into "the funnel," as the width of the straight decreases from 80 to 20 feet (24–6m) over the course of the 200–400-foot (60–120m) section. This forces the riders to take a position in the "field" of riders before entering the first turn.

In Supercross, the first turn is always a left—and it's crucial. As the riders leave the gate simultaneously, they are generally still positioning themselves as they come into the turn, so a few things happen. The front riders, especially the lead rider, have the advantage of getting through cleanly and extending their

EXTREME CONDITIONS. BELOW: RIDERS SCRAMBLE THROUGH A SEA OF MUD WHICH TESTS THE LIMITS OF EVERYBODY; RIGHT: HIGH-FLYER TAKES THE CHEQUERED FLAG AT THE WORLD EXTREME GAMES.

73

lead. But the first turn forces riders in the main pack into one another, and a lot of crashes can occur. A rider can come through clean and get a shot at winning, or lose so much distance in a fall, that winning is virtually impossible.

The obstacles—riders now weave their way through a series of turns that lead them over several obstacles (jumps), ranging from fairly easy to difficult and technicall challenging.

The jumps are designed to challenge a rider's ability to the fullest, create close racing, and maximize airtime. Jumps come in many sizes and are linked to create varying degrees of difficulty throughout he course. The jumps are categorized as:

- SINGLE JUMP – rider jumps 20–60 feet (6–18m) onto a flat landing
- DOUBLE JUMP – rider jumps off one obstacle and lands on the far side of the next, usually covering 20–70 feet (6–21m) of terrain
- TRIPLE JUMP – rider must get through three consecutive jumps and may choose to jump them as sets of two and one, or as a group of three (launching over an entire triple requires the rider to catch up to 25 feet (7.6m) of vertical air over a distance of 75 feet (23m) or more. Triples are real crowd pleasers)
- WHOOPS – a series of short and steep bumps across the width of the course that throw the rider about while crossing them.

The obstacles in Supercross give the riders enough time in the air to read *War And Peace*. Instead, they use the hang time to perform stylish trick maneuvers, many of which were created in BMX. Here are some of them:

- WHIP IT – moving the motorcycle from one side to the other in the air
- PANCAKE – pitching motorcycle and rider over to the side, as close to 90 degrees from vertical as possible
- CANCAN – taking one leg and bringing it across the motorcycle seat to the other side and back before landing
- NAC NAC – taking one leg off the back of the motorcycle and swinging backward to look at what's behind you while in the air. A move made famous by Jeremy McGrath
- HELL CLICKER – an insane move created by Kevin Windham where the rider lifts their feet and clicks their heels together in front of the motorcycle before landing
- BAR HOP – another insane move that's often practiced but unsuitable in a race where the rider takes their feet and places them on the handlebars before landing
- SUPERMAN AIR – another McGrath move where the rider holds on to the handlebars and lets the rest of their body fly up away from the motorcycle while airborne.

The moves and obstacles in the Supercross Series are not natural, but many natural obstacles exist in areas that every rider can get to and play on. The machinery and technology of modern bikes has produced unprecedented opportunities to push the limits. Because the expanse of natural terrain is so broad, and so easily reached on a motoX bike, the only limitation of what can by ridden and how is defined by who's riding it.

One unfortunate aspect of motoX is that riders of all levels of ability and physical strength can get a motoX bike to go fast. As a result, every year riders are injured while performing stunts and tricks they are not prepared to handle, or over terrain they are unfamiliar with. The most important thing to remember for each motorcycle and motoX rider is that it's very easy to go fast and catch a lot of air, but it is not very easy to control and land the motorcycle. Take your time and learn at a reasonable pace; extreme riding requires years of practice, and excellent physical conditioning.

LIVEWIRES. BELOW: MOTOCROSS AT THE WORLD EXTREME GAMES, MELBOURNE, AUSTRALIA, DECEMBER 2000; RIGHT: ACTION FROM THE GP CLASS RACE, MOTOCROSS WORLD CHAMPIONSHIPS.

EXTREME SKIING

THERE WAS A TIME WHEN THE SKI SLOPES WERE OVERLY POLICED, OMINOUSLY WELL ORDERED AND DEVOID OF THE PIONEERING SPIRIT THAT FIRST DREW SKIERS TO THE MOUNTAINS. THEN CAME EXTREME SKIING…

For years skiing has symbolized the carefree pursuit of sport in paradise-like winter settings around the world. Since the first skier rode downhill somewhere in Scandinavia, skiing has drawn free-spirited athletes to the mountains. But enjoyment of the sport became for many a lifestyle statement, and the thrill of challenging terrain and conditions seemed to dwindle. Ski resorts tamed skiing. Snowcats and other terrain-grooming equipment were

TAKING SKIING TO THE LIMITS. LEFT: MICHA BLACK HAS FUN RISING TO THE TOUGH CHALLENGE OF MOUNTAINOUS NEW ZEALAND; BELOW: SOLO SKIER LEAVES A SERPENTINE TRAIL IN HIS WAKE.

introduced along with gentle pistes, vista spots and posh resort restaurants.

Not long ago skiing was a very different pursuit of pioneering and exploration. The reward, and ultimately the feeling of relaxation, came from succeeding in a test of personal ability, courage and stamina. Early skis were more like coasting snowshoes, used for survival and hunting (and undoubtedly fun as well). Then some Nordic skiers—on Nordic or Telemark skis only the toe of the skiers' boot is attached to the ski—tired of fighting their gear on difficult descents, started fixing their heels down to create what would become known as alpine skiing. That in turn led to the

WHO DARES WINS. CLOCKWISE (FROM RIGHT):
YVES DE ROCHE FINDS HIMSELF IN DEEP POWDER AT
GRINDELWALD, SWITZERLAND; DAN WARBICK GETS
AIR; THE SNOW FLIES IN NEW ZEALAND.

first ski lifts, since the whole idea of alpine skiing is to ride down, not up. With the introduction of lifts and easy access to peaks, the mountains became a tourist attraction and the rest, as they say, is history.

Now a new generation of extreme athletes are redefining the meaning of downhill skiing.

Steep descents in the early days of alpine skiing required many of the mountaineering skills that today's top extreme skiers continue to use. Snowshoes, ice picks, crampons and avalanche safety equipment remain standard fare, with the obvious addition of helicopter and snowcat access to remote regions. These new transportation options have expanded the amount of terrain available to extreme skiers, as well as the difficulty of the terrain that can be skied. Slopes of 60 degrees or more are not uncommon for the very best to ski successfully.

Ski, boot, and binding technology has improved dramatically over the years reducing the number of injuries and adding valuable control to skiers who seek out steep terrain. Some resorts even invite skiers to sample lift-served steep skiing as the popularity of extreme skiing grows.

Although alpine skis would seem the most appropriate, they are not always necessary. Alpine touring bindings let skiers free their heels for limited movement, giving them a way to climb without their equipment. But Nordic equipment has also been refined and now gives free-heeled telemark skiers the kind of added control that was not available even in the early days of alpine technology. As a result, many different athletes ski extreme terrain on a broad range of skiing equipment.

Extreme skiing has been widely popularized by filmmakers like Warren Miller and Greg Stump, whose now seminal ski movies of the Eighties showed people the possibilities of extreme skiing. As skiers became more familiar with the types of terrain that were skiable, extreme skiing grew among those who saw skiing as a personal challenge. With the glamorization of extreme skiing and the top experts who featured in those films, more and more skiers started pushing the boundaries of what was possible.

"Going big" means skiing the steepest terrain, dropping off large cliffs, and flying through the air. With top skiers this usually means a controlled landing. With skiers who seek to emulate the top extreme skiers, but haven't yet developed the skills, this means pain. Every year, more and more people are trying out extreme skiing, which inevitably means more casualties. There is also a rise in

FRESH MOUNTAIN AIR. BOTTOM: GEOFF SMALL IN VALDEZ, ALASKA; RIGHT: BEN KIENER FINDS PERFECT CONDITIONS IN SWITZERLAND; FAR RIGHT: KENT KRIETLER AT LAKE OHAU, NEW ZEALAND.

injuries in experts as they strive to progress in an arena that punishes mistakes viciously. The lesson here is that to ski the most difficult terrain on earth an athlete must be able to ski under control no matter how steep the pitch or how big the air. Even the best still get injured and occasionally killed. The best way to build your skills is to practice on short pitches of steep terrain to lessen the consequences.

The European Alps, the North American Rockies, the South American Andes, the Southern Alps of New Zealand and most imposingly the Chugach in Alaska all attract skiers and snowboarders from around the world for extreme mountain adventures each year. Because of this demand an entire industry has sprung up around providing access to steep terrain. Each year thousands of skiers and snowboarders travel to remote mountain peaks for a few thousand vertical feet of untracked terrain, an extreme skier's dream. There are very few things in life that can match the feeling of charging down a steep powder run.

A series of international events focusing on steep-terrain skiing have popped up over the past few years in each of these regions, with the World Championships held each year in Valdez, Alaska. These events are a fantastic showcase for not only the best extreme terrain skiers in the world, but also for some of the most beautiful places in the world. The interest in the events is exploding throughout the skiing world and beyond because of both the challenge and scenery these events offer.

Extreme skiing is the last frontier of modern skiing; it fills the void for skiers who no longer find skiing in resort backcountry to be as exciting as it was. As skiing extreme regions becomes more and more popular, expect to find a lot more folks heading to steeper challenges of technical terrain.

FREESTYLE SKIING

THE SKIING FRATERNITY DID NOT AT FIRST WELCOME THE ARRIVAL OF SNOWBOARDING IN THE LATE EIGHTIES. IT WAS TO BE THE START OF A PERIOD OF CHANGE FOR THE CONSERVATIVE SKIING ENVIRONMENT.

Fast forward to the mid-Nineties and the acceptance of snowboarding as a legitimate alpine sport came about. The realization that it had revolutionized the way people looked at the mountain meant that skiers couldn't ignore it. Despite the media playing on the conflict between skiing and snowboarding, the reality was that skiers and snowboarders were riding together. It was to become a unity that would spawn a new form of skiing.

Freestyle skiing is one of many sports that have entered the extreme sports world in the last 10 years as a diversification from an existing sport. Taking its lead from snowboarding, freestyle skiing was born in the snowboard parks that sprang up all over the mountains to cater for the needs of skateboard-oriented snowboarders. Young skiers started to copy the moves that snowboarders were pulling; the traditional skiing style of having the ankles together gave way to a much more functional wide stance and freestyle skiers started to wear the baggy loose-fitting clothes that snowboarders had brought to the mountains.

The main factors that have given rise to the naming of a new sport, or at least a new genre of a sport, are obviously not just where people ride and what they wear. The main revolution took place in the equipment. Skiers who were riding with snowboarders realized that it was just as easy to go backward as it was forward. Soon ski companies were developing prototype twin-tip skis that could perform equally well in either direction. Boots were made with more lateral flex to allow the skiers more maneuverability.

The next piece of the puzzle was the adaptation of snowboard and skateboarding tricks to skis. Soon skiers were grabbing their skis in the air for stability and style and inventing quite a few of their own moves along the way. Probably the most surprising was skiing's exploration of the urban environment of hand rails. This is a realm that sits at the heart of street skateboarding and urban snowboarding and, for a sport previously as conservative as skiing, to explore this side of the sport was significant progress.

While the skiers pushed back the boundaries on the mountains, so the designers set to work in the factories. Various combinations of skis were tested; snow blades were developed along the same lines as the roller blade but they were too unstable for landing big jumps (they still stand as a great learning tool for kids and great fun for adults).

FLYING THROUGH THE AIR WITH THE GREATEST OF EASE. RIGHT: THE FRENCH FREESTYLE SKIING CHAMPIONSHIP, VARS, 2001; BELOW: IT CAN BE EXCITING TAKING THE AIR UP IN THE MOUNTAINS.

NO LIMITS. CLOCKWISE (FROM TOP RIGHT): LOOPING THE LOOP; CRASHING THROUGH THE FRAME IN THE FRENCH ALPS; COMPETITOR IN THE FRENCH CHAMPIONSHIPS, VARS, 2001.

For a while, traditional poles were discarded by some in favor of a hands-free approach that drew the young sport even closer to snowboarding. But poles were reinstated for the next move this fledgling sport would make.

At the same time as the twin tip skis were being developed so were "fat boys." Designed with a lot of surface area for the larger-than-average human to float in soft powder snow, it soon became apparent that a normal-sized person could also benefit from having these wider skis.

This had always been the biggest gap between snowboarding and freestyle skiing: the huge surface area of snowboards meant that they would glide on the surface of soft powder snow where skis would become slow and cumbersome. This innovation allowed skiers to float like snowboarders and that meant that freestyle skiing would be able to move into the backcountry.

Taking the tricks they had learnt in the snow parks of resorts, freestyle skiers moved into the backcountry wilderness around the resorts to build bigger jumps using natural terrain.

In the same way that street skating created a video culture in skateboarding, so has back-country snowboarding and skiing. There are now around 10 videos released every season documenting the progression of the sport as well as magazine titles in most countries. Probably the best acceptance for the sport has come through the unlikely channel of competition where freestyle skiing is now a regular event at both the Winter X Games and the Gravity Games.

It is possible to argue that freestyle skiing is actually just the logical progression and modernization of hot dog skiing that arrived in the first boom of skiing in the Seventies and referred to the all-mountain style of jumps and turns that young skiers of the day were into.

There are also roots in the established (and Olympics-endorsed) form of freestyle skiing that translates as a form of aerial gymnastics on skis.

Both of these had been around for decades and have without question helped freestyle skiing progress—but without snowboarding as the inspiration we might still be waiting for the revolution that has changed the way that young skiers look at the mountain.

The best irony for freestyle skiers is that the once outlaw reputation of snowboarding has been cleaned up by its acceptance into the Olympics, while, as far as the freestylers are concerned, they can leave that side of skiing to the racers.

LAND & ICE YACHTING

LAND SAILING BEGAN HUNDREDS OF YEARS AGO IN CHINA WHEN IT WAS DISCOVERED THAT THE POWER OF THE WIND COULD BE HARNESSED TO MAKE TASKS LIKE PLOWING AND MOVING OBJECTS EASIER. RECENT DEVELOPMENTS IN THIS AREA BEGAN WHEN SOMEONE DECIDED IT WOULD MAKE A FUN SPORT.

Modern land yachts are capable of attaining speeds exceeding 100 mph (160kph)—the world record is 116 mph (185kph). Many modern land yachts are designed to swap out their wheels in the winter for ice blades. Ice yachts, with less friction to inhibit their speed, are now exceeding 150 mph (240kph). Land and ice sailing designs are generally limited to modern three-wheel machines. There are some other approaches to land and ice sailing, such as skateboard-like systems employing either wheels or blades mounted to windsurfer rigs. These systems do not reach the velocities of their larger counterparts, but are nonetheless exciting and challenging to sail.

Landsailing can be practiced on a broad range of surfaces. The dry lake beds of the U.S.A. are a favorite of landsailors globally. Abandoned airfields are a great site for sailing, however they are more temperamental, since the asphalt direction and the wind direction don't always line up just right. Many land sailing enthusiasts enjoy sailing on beaches, which often offer a predictable breeze that is perpendicular to the required direction of travel, the preferred wind direction for beach sailing.

Ice yachts have a slightly easier time finding suitable ice to sail on. Their primary problem is finding lakes that are sizable enough to allow them to not only accelerate up to speed, but also to turn safely before coming ashore. There are techniques for spilling the air that allow the sailor to somewhat lower their terminal velocity, however, those techniques rely on the yacht not changing direction away from the wind's quadrant because doing so will change their apparent wind and accelerate their yacht.

Both land and ice yachts must deal with the concept of apparent wind when negotiating the terrain's limitations. Perhaps the easiest way to explain apparent wind would be to park your car so that the wind is hitting it at 90 degrees to the driver's door. If you were to take a reading on the direction of a wind blowing at 20 mph (32kph) as it hit the door, the apparent wind would equal 20 mph at 90 degrees. If you then accelerated away to 20 mph, your apparent wind would increase to reflect the speed you were traveling versus the 20 mph wind hitting the side of your car. The angle of the apparent wind also changes to roughly 45 degrees forward of the driver's side. If you were to turn your car, both the angle and the speed of the apparent wind would change with you.

If understanding apparent wind seems complicated, it is. To drive a land or ice yacht at high speeds of 100+ mph, requires total driver control. A poor driver is a risk to other sailors and to themselves. Striking another vehicle traveling at 100 mph when you are also traveling at 100 mph is certainly not something any sane person would want to do. Focus and lightning reflexes mean the difference between a good day and a ride to the hospital.

Reflexes are not always good enough. Imagine sailing an ice boat at 150 mph (240kph) and hitting a raised crack in the ice. This does happen, and the results are rarely painless. Many ice sailors have had severe leg injuries and been killed in such instances. Land sailors have similar concerns, especially that of "capsizing" (tipping over) their craft. Unlike ice boats, which can slide through such an event, land yachts that capsize crash hard. Land yachts also run the risk of hitting unseen, or unforeseen objects at high speed, especially on dry lake beds.

Modern land and ice boaters are constantly seeking new technologies to make their yachts both faster and safer. The use of composite materials together with modular construction techniques have helped to make the yachts lighter and better able to withstand impacts due to either capsize or striking

GLIDING ACROSS SAND AND ICE. LEFT: DRIVING LAND OR ICE YACHTS REQUIRES TOTAL DRIVER CONTROL: BELOW: RED SAILS IN THE SUNSET AS COMPETITORS PICK UP MOMENTUM IN A LAND YACHT RACE.

debris. However, it is questionable if a remedy can be created for high speed collisions.

One of the most exciting high-tech modifications is the removal of the old wire "stayed" mast systems for hoisting the sails that power these yachts. New technology is replacing soft sails with hard adjustable wing designs that are lighter, more efficient, and allow for greater velocity. Wings are more easily "tuned" to either accelerate or decelerate the yachts, and the lift they generate to move the yacht can be positioned so as to effectively place the yacht into an "idle" mode.

The first recorded use of a land-sailing vehicle was around 1600 when Flemish engineer Simon Stevin created a massive two-masted land yacht for beach travel. The yacht could carry a group of 28 passengers at speeds exceeding 20 mph.

In the nineteenth century many attempts were made to create a sail-powered vehicle for transportation purposes. One of the more famous attempts was in the U.S., where the Baltimore and Ohio Railroad successfully used a special sailing railcar to transport, among others, the Russian Ambassador, who subsequently requested one for the Czar. Later around the time of the California Gold Rush in 1849, many settlers and prospectors heading across the plains attached sails to Contessa Wagons, enabling them to travel further and faster than without the aid of wind power. These wagons did, however, have some substantial handling problems, as their extinction would indicate.

One thing is for sure, even if land and ice yachts are now only reserved for extreme sports enthusiasts, the opportunity to harness the wind in order to travel will always exist, and the urge to push the limits of performance will continue to redefine these exciting and dangerous sports.

MOUNTAIN BIKING

CHARGING DOWN A HILL AT WARP SPEED ON A BIKE IS A RUSH THAT MOST OF US HAVE ENJOYED AT SOME TIME OR OTHER. AS BIKES DEVELOPED THEY HEADED DOWN THE PATH OF TRADITION AND, FOR A WHILE, ALL A BIKE BUYER COULD FIND WAS A ROAD-RACING-STYLE BIKE OR A CRUISER. THEN CAME SOMETHING NEW.

Road bikes were fine for speed and offered a broad range of gears. But road bikes offered little comfort and didn't take very well to rough surfaces. Cruisers were very comfortable, but heavy and not geared very well. All that changed in the early Eighties when a Japanese bike company by the name of Specialized purchased a unique bike made in Marin County, California and took it home for a closer look.

The mountain bike can trace its roots back to when a small and unknown group of riders in Marin County first began riding stripped down and beefed up Schwinns on mountain roads just prior to WWII. One can only assume that the natural propensity of extreme oriented riders continued to pursue downhill riding until a few notable pioneers of the modern mountain bike began simultan-eously experimenting and redefining the equipment they were riding.

According to one of those pioneers, Gary Fischer, the early Schwinn "Ballooner" Cruiser bikes everyone was riding were so heavy that they were pushed, not ridden, uphill. Fischer is reported to have been the first to equip a Ballooner with multiple gears, an act that made it easier to pedal uphill, but also added 25 lbs (11.35kg) to their weight.

Racing provided inspiration for many of the upgrades that are now taken for granted on modern mountain bikes. Not suprisingly, most of the advances in mountain biking took place after the first official mountain bike race took place on 21 October, 1976. The racers on the 2.1 mile (3.4km) course down Mt. Tamalpais could not possibly have known the biking revolution they were starting that day. The race was dubbed the Repack since the brakes required repacking after each heat due

THROUGH MUD, WIND AND THROUGH RAIN.
BELOW: CANADIAN OLYMPIAN ANDREAS HESTER;
RIGHT: JOSH BENDER "GOES HUGE" IN THE
RED BULL RAMPAGE, VIRGIN, UTAH.

to the extreme pitch. Repack organizer Charlie Kelly was reported to have considered the race so extreme that he couldn't imagine many riders would get into it for very long.

In 1977, pioneer racer and bike builder Joe Breeze became the first to build a mountain bike from the stiffer and lighter chrome-moly materials used in road-racing bikes. To that he added the most lightweight and rugged components, giving birth to the first modern mountain bike. Five years later in 1983, Specialized would release its StumpJumper, the first mass-produced mountain bike made commercially available.

The release and overwhelming success of the StumpJumper fueled an explosion of demand for the new-style mountain bikes. Recreational riders had long been turned off by the dropped-style handlebars on all standard road bikes. The mountain bikes were so rugged and versatile that they could be ridden anywhere. Amazingly, sales of mountain bikes grew to surpass the sale of road bikes by 1986, and an entire global industry was born.

The surge in sales demanded an entirely new set of accessories that were mountain bike specific. The balloon tires of the early Schwinns were replaced by "nobby, fat" tires that looked more like motocross tires than the skinny road tires on the bikes they quickly replaced. Road-style, swept down handlebars were replaced by straight handlebars that were more comfortable. The saddles became more comfortable, too. A broader seating surface and padding, versus traditional road bike hard saddles, made the comfort package complete. The sum of fatter tires, straight handlebars, and softer saddles made converts out of riders who couldn't have cared less that the bikes they were buying could climb steep hills and fly down at high speed with great control.

More accessories were added and new approaches to old needs created. Riders soon discovered that the addition of bar ends could allow them to shift their weight forward and upward in climbing situations. Bar ends are short sections of tubing, either straight or curved, that attach to the end of the handlebars at an angle of roughly 90 degrees. They were soon a requirement for racing, and many mountain bikers who didn't race got them as well. New clip in pedal systems were created with mountain bikers in mind, replacing the strapped in toe clip-style retainers that didn't let a rider separate from their bike in a fall.

Innovation and competition continued to fuel the growth of mountain biking. Since Gary Fischer and Joe Breeze's first

MOUNTAIN BIKES HAVE OPENED UP EXTREME TERRAIN EVEN FOR RECREATIONAL RIDERS AND FAMILY OUTINGS, BUT THERE ARE SOME THINGS THAT ONLY THE PROS SHOULD ATTEMPT.

modifications in the Seventies, mountain bikes have been produced in a number of materials and frame styles, each focused on specific competitive needs. Materials now range from the chrome-moly in Joe Breeze's 1977 frame to aluminum, titanium, and space-age ceramic and composite materials.

The original one front sprocket (gear) and one rear sprocket single-gear set up gave way to three front and eight rear sprockets as gearing went from 1-speed to 3, to 10, to 15, to 18, to 21, to the highest currently available— 24-speed gearing. Frame sets went from rigid to suspension forks with the introduction of the Rock Shock fork system. Soon, rear suspension was the rage, and full-suspension bikes continue to redefine performance on downhill and slalom courses. Now downhill racing bikes are created with full suspension in mind at the beginning of the design stage, not as an add-on feature. Suspension travel on some of the more radical designs exceeds 12 inches in the front and rear, allowing for massive shock absorbtion at high speeds, increased tire contact at speed, and higher top end velocities. Downhill racers spent most of their time in "loose" tracking stances in early racing, with their rear tires drifting and their bikes constantly on the edge of control. Suspensions allow the riders to "carve" their turns now, using the suspension and their bodies to keep the tires locked into the terrain they are riding. New disciplines of mountain bike racing have evolved from mountain biking's popularity:

- CROSS COUNTRY RACING pits competitors against each other and the clock for best overall finish on a closed and gated course over grueling, technical terrain. Cross country became an Olympic medal sport in 1996, replacing the dated road team time trial event.
- DOWNHILL RACING pits riders against the clock for best descent through a closed and gated course. The eliminator race pits rider against rider for a best score of two runs. Speeds often exceed 60 mph (97kph) and crashes are dramatic and painful.
- DUAL SLALOM racing pits rider against rider on a closed gated course that requires the riders to execute a number of tight turns successfully on the way to the finish.
- OBSERVED TRIALS events require riders to complete a course consisting of obstacles and hazards. The riders must complete the course without "dabbing" (putting their feet down for balance). Riders are penalized by adding points for each dab. The rider with the least points wins.

• UPHILL RACING is a timed competition of sustained climbing where competitors finish at altitudes higher than where they started.

While all of these types of racing and styles of bikes have emerged during mountain biking's rapid evolution, the underlying allure of the kind of riding these bikes have allowed us to enjoy has not. The images and beauty of the outdoors are really why mountain biking has grown so rapidly. Mountain bikes have opened up an entire range of remote wilderness and landscapes that recreational trail hikers had never been able to get to so easily or quickly. Not surprisingly, many of the most popular mountain biking regions are established hiking areas.

With the emergence of bikes on hiking terrain came territorial issues of who should and shouldn't have access to the trails.

Not surprisingly hikers complained that mountain bikers weren't environmentally friendly enough to the trails, and were leaving trash and erosion problems behind them as they rode. Many of these complaints were justified, and organizations like the International Mountain Biking Association (IMBA) and the National Off Road Bicycle Association (NORBA) in the U.S. have worked hard to educate their members in order to decrease the impact mountain biking can have on the environment and on trails. Mountain bikes quickly reshaped the inner city messenger business, too. Urban dwellers and travelers can't help notice the volumes of bike messengers in virtually every city in the world. Modern cities are filled with hundreds of riders constantly riding through traffic, over kerbs and stairs, and through parks in a quest for timely delivery. Not surprisingly, many of these riders are competing or aspiring professional mountain bike racers.

GET THE HEART RATE GOING. NEAR RIGHT: COMPETITIVE MOUNTAIN BIKING HAS BECOME MORE AND MORE POPULAR; FAR RIGHT: WILD ACTION FROM THE RED BULL RAMPAGE, VIRGIN, UTAH.

MOUNTAINBOARDING

MOUNTAINBOARDING IS A RELATIVE NEWCOMER TO THE WORLD OF EXTREME SPORTS, ALTHOUGH IT IS POSSIBLE TO TRACK ITS LINEAGE TO SOME OF THE OTHER MORE "ESTABLISHED" EXTREME SPORTS SUCH AS SNOWBOARDING AND MOUNTAIN BIKING.

Essentially, the mountainboard creators developed a hybrid skateboard/snowboard that allows aspects of each sport to be used on terrain where neither can be practiced. Which isn't to say that skateboarders have not tried using fat tires on their skateboards so that they can ride on loose sand and gravel—they have. Snowboarders also discovered that their boards can be made to double as sand surfers. However, until the mountainboard the only way to travel downhill at speed on a mountain road, over rocks, or gravel was on a mountain bike.

The name Mountainboard is a registered trademark of the Mountainboard company in Colorado Springs, Colorado. The company is owned by creators Patrick McConnell and Jason Lee, two Vail snowboarders who developed the board as a way to ride Vail during the summer as a cross-training tool for winter riding.

The two soon discovered that the design rode so well that friends were buying as many as they could make, and a business was born from the idea.

Another athlete on another continent created a similar vehicle at just about the same time. Australian surfer John Miln developed a three-wheeled board (the Mountainboard uses four) using a different steering set-up a short while before the Vail snowboarders begun. The Outback Mountainboard design uses two wheels in front to steer the rig and one at the back, and includes a brake.

Both systems are steered just like a skateboard, by leaning the board's deck in the required direction. On dirt and loose surfaces, the boards respond much like a snowboard. Riders can drive the rear of the board hard into the turn, "scrubbing" (slowing) their speed by getting the rear of the board slightly loose in the turn.

On hard surfaces like pavement, they roll faster with fully-inflated tires, and slower on soft tires. This means that the rider stops just

like a skateboarder—by getting off. They are said to be highly stable and controllable with practice.

While only a single model of the Outback is available, the rival Mountainboards are available in a variety of lengths, just like a snowboard. Shorter versions are for freestyle riding, while the longer ones offer better directional stability and are better suited to speed riding. Both take a range of tires, from slick pavement tires to knobby dirt tires.

Competition will determine the better board. With new competition from Mongoose, and continuous improvements, such as new braking systems and lighter components, it appears that Mountainboard's four wheel version is where the market is headed.

Whichever wins the consumers' hearts in the end, there is no doubt that mountainboards are here to stay.

Extreme athletes and enthusiasts will certainly take the opportunity to redefine what can be done on pavement or dirt, it only takes a few creative athletes to establish a new way to have fun doing it.

MOUNTAINBOARDING IS BEGINNING TO CATCH ON. BELOW: SILHOUETTE OF A TIRED BUT HAPPY MOUNTAINBOARDER; TOP RIGHT: JOHN WHITE AT SLICK ROCK, UTAH, ONE OF THE TOP MOUNTAIN-BOARD SITES; BELOW RIGHT: BIG AIR ON A BOARD.

OUTDOOR CLIMBING

MOUNTAIN CLIMBING IS AS OLD AS MANKIND. IT HAS NOT ALWAYS BEEN A "SPORT," PERHAPS IT WAS BETTER CLASSIFIED AS A SURVIVAL SKILL. WHILE MOUNTAIN CLIMBING IS THE ACT OF ASCENDING A MOUNTAIN UNDER YOUR OWN POWER, EXTREME MOUNTAIN CLIMBING IS HARDLY A LEISURE ACTIVITY.

Climbing mountains covers two basic categories, technical and non-technical. The latter requires little more than sheer energy and knowledge of one's own limitations. No special equipment, just a good rugged and supportive pair of hiking shoes. Technical climbing requires the use of ropes and other specialized equipment to ascend the terrain to be climbed. The equipment is used so that, in the event of a fall, the climber is both protected from injury and securely fastened to the rock or ice.

Technical climbing can be broken into two components, ice and rock. Rock climbing involves scaling cliffs and boulders in situations that could prove hazardous or dangerous.

The most extreme rock climbers can scale the rock without the use of equipment beyond their shoes and some chalk to aid them grip the rock. These climbers "solo" their way up the faces of cliffs that are a match for many expert climbers even when they are using ropes or gear to attach them to the mountain in the event of a fall. Because extreme solo climbers ascend without these aids, solo climbers are either very good, or very dead.

Ice climbing entails scaling cliffs and boulders that are entirely covered with ice and snow. Climbing ice requires an additional level of specialized equipment such as "crampons," the metal spikes which ice climbers attach to the bottom of their climbing shoes. In ice climbing, even the most proficient extreme climbers require the aid of equipment that allows them to grip the ice and snow without slipping.

Extreme climbers must be familiar with all the technical gear, and must spend substantial time "on the rock" to successfully undertake those difficult climbs requiring highly specialized technique. The most difficult terrain demands a level of physical conditioning and

SCALING THE HEIGHTS. ABOVE AND RIGHT: THERE'S NO FEELING LIKE GETTING TO THE TOP OF A MOUNTAIN UNDER YOUR OWN STEAM.

mental toughness that few sports require. An extreme climber who has command of their body, mind, and surroundings can be considered relatively safe in conditions that "normal" people would consider perilous.

Serious climbers do not "solo" (or climb alone). Climbing requires teamwork and a focus on not just personal safety, but the safety of the other climbers. Because climbers constantly rely on others to ensure their safety, it is important that everyone is aware of not only their personal limitations, but of those they are with as well.

Extreme mountain climbing ascents like Mount Everest or K2 are world famous not only for the climbers who have successfully reached their peaks, but also for the many who have failed or died in the process of the climb. To successfully climb peaks of this level of difficulty requires months of planning and a team of tremendous talent. Top expert abilities in both ice and rock climbing are essential requirements for those considering attempting an extreme mountain ascent. Each team of climbers that reaches the top can point to their climbing team members as well as dozens of support people at different stages of the climb, without whom the climb would have failed.

A complete knowledge of life-saving and first-aid skills are also much needed assets in each team member. With the extreme altitude of these climbs, abrupt weather changes can strand an injured climber on the mountain for days before rescue is possible. Without sufficient first aid, a climber can die before outside assistance is made available. Because temperatures can quickly drop off the scale, advanced life-saving protective gear is also required, and must be available during the entire ascent and descent.

Most climbing is not, however, done in remote areas on massive peaks. It takes place within hours of major urban areas and towns around the globe. The fact that many climbing

102

areas are accessible does not make them any less extreme. A simple categorization system has been created in every country to classify the difficulty of a climb. In France the system uses a series of numbers and letters; in England ascents are graded on difficulty and danger; in the U.S. climbers use what is termed the "Yosemite scale" to help explain the various levels of difficulty climbers can attempt. The Yosemite grading system uses the following structure for each climb:

- CLASS I – Hiking, where most any footwear is considered adequate
- CLASS II – Proper footwear is required for rough terrain and the use of handholds may be needed in some portions of the ascent
- CLASS III – "Scrambling" on hands and feet when use of the hands is required frequently. Ropes should be available if needed
- CLASS IV – Ropes and belays (the system of using ropes between climbers) must be used continuously for safety. Belay anchors may be necessary. (Class IV climbs differ from Class III in that the terrain immediately adjacent to the climb is treacherous and a fall in that direction can be deadly.)
- CLASS V – Leader protection (anchors to secure the rope) required above the belayer
- CLASS VI – Direct aids must be used

Climbs at Class V use a decimal system to detail the difficulty of the climb. The current top, which is of course open to opinion, is somewhere around a V.15. Once climbers get into Class VI, a scale of A0–A6 is used to detail the difficulty of this level.

- A0 – Climb requires use of pre-existing aids (climber not required to place the assistance themselves)
- A1 – Climb requires use of "chocks" (cam devices that anchor into openings in the rock) that are easy to place
- A2 – Climb requires the use of chocks that are difficult to place
- A3 – Climb requires the installation of a

hook into the rock because chock placement is not possible
- A4 – Very "sketchy," aids used where the likelihood of the aid holding in the event of a fall is not high, very risky climbing
- A5 – Extremely sketchy
- A6 – So sketchy, the likelihood of A6 levels being climbable is debatable

Other terms used in climbing:

- PITON – metal blades or angles with an open eye at the blunt end which are driven into cracks in the rock to secure belays and leader protection
- CARABINER – snaplinks of varying sizes and shapes used for connecting climbing rope with a piton, sling, or chock. These are made with either a "non-locking" spring gate closure or "locking" screw lock mechanism
- ROUTE – a path up the rock where the ascent is made
- FLASH – successfully climbing a to the top of a route without falling
- ON-SIGHT – attempting to climb a route without any previous information or guidance
- WHIP OR AIRTIME – a long fall (all long falls stop suddenly whether the rope holds or not)
- OVERHANG – a portion of the rock which stretches upward past the vertical
- ROOF – a severe overhang requiring upside down climbing
- BUCKET – a very good hold
- SMEAR – holding on to the rock using friction from the climbers rubber footwear
- LUNGE – climber throws him or herself at an out of reach hold (missing the hold means a fall)
- BARNDOOR – an out of balance climber swinging away from the rock
- FLAG – using a free leg as a counterbalance to maintain control during a barndoor.

BELOW: SHEER FACE; RIGHT: ICE CLIMBING IS A TRUE TEST OF ENDURANCE; FAR RIGHT: PATRICK EDLINGER SOLOS UP THE SUGAR LOAF MOUNTAIN, BRAZIL.

104

SKATEBOARDING

WITHOUT QUESTION, SKATEBOARDING EPITOMIZES EXTREME SPORTS AT THEIR MOST RADICAL. WITH ITS OWN NOISE, FASHIONS AND ATTITUDE, SKATEBOARDING CONTINUES TO REDEFINE ITSELF, CONSTANTLY PUSHING THE LIMITS OF WHAT CAN BE DONE PHYSICALLY, MENTALLY AND EVEN CULTURALLY.

Skateboarding is without question one of the most technically difficult sports on earth to master, even the beginner must endure weeks of practice before mastering the most basic tricks. It is a hugely creative sport that still has a highly individualistic approach 40 years on from its birth, making it one of the most progressive extreme sports of all.

Although no one can take the credit for officially inventing the skateboard, its origins are easy to trace. The first skateboard was a simplified version of a child's toy, the push-scooter. Push-scooters were popular toys in the Fifties, made from dismantled roller skates nailed to a plank that you stood on with a crate attached as a balance aid. Remove the crate, and you have a skateboard.

A wave of new technology, a natural phenomenon and a glut of fresh talent in the early Seventies redefined the sport's limits. The use of the petroleum-based compound polyurethane made faster, grippier wheels, and a drought in California in the summer of 1972 provided an oasis of dried-out swimming pools. Meanwhile, a new aggressive surfing style coming out of Hawaii influenced a fresh crop of young skaters to emulate their water-based maneuvers on these walls of curved concrete.

Together these advances put skateboarding at the forefront of youth culture

and in the Seventies skateboarding boomed. By the end of the decade there were hundreds of skate parks, millions of skaters, and an industry was born. Pool skating was the chosen terrain of the Seventies and dominates the images of early skateboarding.

Names like Tony Alva, Jay Adams, and Stacy Peralta appeared as heroes of skateboarding's second wave. But every boom has a bust and the meteoric rise gave way to a decline in popularity due to inflated skate park admission fees and insurance issues. Many skate parks and manufacturers went bust. But hardcore skaters persevered, building backyard ramps and, as the skateparks closed, they turned to the streets as a new environment in which to develop their skills.

In the early Eighties skateboarding began to rise again in the U.S. Soon skaters in other countries began following suit, and skateboarders worldwide began pushing their collective boundaries. It was the dawn of the video age and, inspired by early videos of the Bones Brigade Skaters like Tony Hawk and Steve Caballero, kids all over the world could suddenly emulate their heroes. Stacy Peralta, the one time world champion and an original pioneer of the Seventies skate scene, was the brains behind Powell Peralta skateboards, and using the medium of video he masterminded a global profile for skateboarding.

He took the Bones Brigade on world tours to inspire skaters in every country; the best testament to his work is the fact that the talent he assembled on one team still lead their chosen disciplines almost 20 years after he brought them together. Tony Hawk is arguably the best vert skater in the world, if not the most famous extreme icon; Danny Way has gone on to break numerous world records and become quite possibly the most progressive athlete of the twenty-first century. These people have inspired millions of kids, which has created another generation of hugely creative skaters. It is this constant process of evolution that has made skateboarding such an influence on so many other sports.

Skating can be linked directly to snowboarding, which has borrowed the half-pipe and many of skateboarding's moves and style. Skateboarding techniques can be seen in modern surfing style with its jumps and re-entry moves. Skateboarding is especially evident in the progression of inline skating, which has taken much of the style and culture of skateboarding and sought to make it its

CHAIRMEN OF THE BOARD. FROM THE LEFT: THE LEGENDARY STEVE CABALLERO PERFORMS A MASSIVE BACKSIDE AIR; TREVOR WARD IN THE HALF-PIPE AT BELLS BEACH, AUSTRALIA; ANDY MACDONALD GETS AIR IN AN OUTDOOR SKATE BOWL.

own. Wakeboarding finds many of its roots in skateboarding. Street luge is the most direct relative of skateboarding, and in fact got its start from folks lying down and going fast on skateboard before the term street luge was even coined.

Skateboarding is now growing internationally and faster than ever. Skating is one of only a handful of sports that has been embraced by young people globally. The top athletes in skateboarding are renowned worldwide within skateboarding circles and mainstream media. To put it in perspective, Tony Hawk has the best selling PlayStation game ever and in 2003 made more money than Michael Jordan.

The sport is quickly moving out of the underground and into the mainstream, just as it did before its last boom. Yet, it is fair to point out that there are forces in place now that should serve to keep skateboarding alive and well for quite some time. After the last boom all the corporate companies who had invested in the sports hardware manufacturers pulled out and left the sport with nothing. It was almost impossible to buy skateboards at one stage in the early Eighties.

Saviors were on hand though; the skaters who had done well out of the boom years invested in new companies that understood skaters and their needs. As the Eighties boom took off, the corporate companies found that there was no room for their products and they were forced out of the market place. It is one of the reasons that skaters are so defensive about their passion, but it serves to protect them from the boom/bust culture of corporate marketing and fads. Even now the steady rise of skateboarding is down to the numerous ageing skaters who are behind most of the successful companies.

Today's skateboarding is a huge mixture of different styles and obstacles. Ramp skateboarding takes place on transitions, the basic idea is to roll backwards and forwards in the U-shaped pipe using your legs to pump and maintain speed. There is a steel pipe called coping that runs along the lip of the ramp and serves to help skaters grind, slide and pop into the air.

Ramps come in all different shapes and sizes from 3ft (1m) high micro minis that are easy to ride and great fun for kids and adults because the angle only reaches 45° at the lip, right up to 15ft (5m) high super ramps that have 2ft (60cm) of vertical at the top. Ramp skating is a refined art that most people only get into if they have facilities close by.

The two most common disciplines in skateboarding are park skating and street skating. Street skating takes place on the streets and this is the secret to the massive appeal of skating today, anyone can skate street at

anytime, anywhere. All you need is a board, a curb and your imagination. The thousands of tricks that have been invented can be combined or modified by an individual's style to create something totally original.

The added bonus of urbanization and modern architecture just serves to enlarge the playground on a daily basis, offering infinite possibilities. The other form of skating is park. Skate parks can take almost any form depending on what they are made out of, whether they are indoors or outdoors, designed by skaters, BMXers or very often contracted builders without a clue.

Concrete was the favored surface of the Seventies and many remain today with their beautiful bowls where speed can be maintained throughout the park by pumping lines around the bowls. In countries, where the weather is harsh, concrete is still used as the most hardwearing surface. Most parks these days are indoor facilities that provide an alternative to street skating when the rain sets in. They are usually built out of wood and have a mixture of flat banks, transitioned ramps, blocks and rails. They are the most common forms of obstacles used when street competitions are set up and some skaters prefer the consistency and speed offered by park skating.

Pools have generally been regarded as the Holy Grail of skate spots for skaters since skateboarding discovered them in the Seventies. Generally, any pool left empty and accessible (by virtually any means) is fair game for skating. With a wide variety of shapes, transitions, and depths, pools are extremely challenging to skate. Pool skating has influenced the construction and design of bowls specifically for skating and was the idea behind the construction of the first ramps. Bowls, constructed of either concrete or wood, generally pay homage to pools through choice of shape, either figure eights or kidney-shaped, and some even replace the metal coping bar with original concrete pool tiles.

All skateboards are essentially the same shape and share the same basic components. Each skateboard has a deck, which is the platform the skater stands on. Decks have been made of fibreglass and plastic, but are almost always made of plywood these days.

Each board has a front, or "nose" and a back, or a "tail." Mounted on the bottom of every deck is a set of "trucks." Trucks are the steering and axle assemblies on which two wheels are mounted. Trucks are available in a variety of widths for different weights and

NEVER FORGET YOUR WHEELS, YOU NEVER KNOW WHEN YOU'LL NEED THEM. RIGHT: SKATER GOING OVER A LONG HAND RAIL. FAR RIGHT: TONY HAWK HANGS ON IN THE HALF-PIPE.

108

stability. Wheels are available in a wide array of width diameters and also in different compounds. Compounds vary by their hardness and traction, generally, harder wheels offer less traction than softer wheels. Each skater has their own preference when it comes to compound, but a general rule is that ramp skating requires larger wheels (56–60mm) and street skating uses smaller wheels (50–56mm).

There are two basic types of skateboards: normal street and vert decks and longboards. The classic street decks are designed to be light and easy to throw around; vert decks are exactly the same except they are a little wider for more stability. Longboards are as you might expect longer than normal decks and tend to use wide trucks for added stability and tracking at speed.

There are two ways to stand on a skateboard. A "regular" stance means that the skater places his left foot on the front of the board. A "goofy foot" means that the skater places his right foot on the front of the board.

Skateboarders have created an almost entirely new language to describe the aerials, slides, grinds, flips and even wheelies that they do. Here are a few of the basic terms to get you started:

- OLLIE – jumping with the board by cracking the tail of the board on the ground and then guiding it through the air using your front foot
- MANUAL – a wheelie on the back wheels
- NOSE MANUAL – a wheelie on the front wheels
- BOARDSLIDE – sliding on a rail or bar on the middle of the deck
- 50/50 – grinding on the trucks
- NOSESLIDE – sliding on the nose of the board
- TAILSLIDE – sliding on the tail of the board
- KICKFLIP – doing an Ollie and, as your front foot guides the board upward, you flick it with your toes, so that the board does a 360° spiral like a torpedo under your feet
- HEELFLIP – exactly the same as a kickflip but you use your heel instead of your toes.
- DROP-IN – putting your tail on the coping of a ramp and then stepping on the front of the board to enter the ramp
- SHOVE-IT – an Ollie where the back foot spins the board 180° under your feet so that the nose becomes the tail when you land
- FAKIE – riding backwards on your board
- SWITCH – changing your stance to goofy if you are regular and regular if you are goofy. Learning switch is a bit like learning to write with your left hand if you are right-handed.

SNOWBOARDING

WITH THE ADVENT OF CHEAP INTERNATIONAL AIR TRAVEL, SKIING AS A SPORT FOR THE MASSES PROGRESSED UNTIL IT REACHED SATURATION POINT—INTEREST AND PARTICIPATION WANED. AND THEN THE ETERNAL SEARCH ETHIC OF THE SURFER-SKATEBOARDER AXIS SAW SNOW GLINTING ON DISTANT HILLS...

In 1965 a Michigan industrial gases engineer began toying with a design that would wind up saving the entire ski industry some 25 years later. Sherman Poppen noticed his daughter attempting to stand on her sledge on the neighbourhood hill.

This inspired him to go to his garage, where he took a pair of children's skis and screwed them together with dowels, which he described as acting like "foot stops." His daughter Wendy took the "sled" to the hill and rode it. When the other kids saw what her dad had created, they all wanted him to build one for them too. He did and they were an instant hit.

Poppen's wife mixed the words surfer and snow together to coin the name "Snurfer," and a product was born. Poppen manufactured Snurfers and distributed them through sporting goods and toy stores, and over the next ten years sold millions. It was the Snurfer that would inspire snowboarding pioneers like Jake Burton Carpenter to develop and manufacture designs that led to the modern snowboard in use by millions of riders today.

Early converts to snowboard riding found a sensation that inspired others to give snowboarding a try. The feeling of riding a snowboard has been described in many different ways, but perhaps the best term is "soulful." Just as skateboarding and surfing have a Zen-like quality to them, snowboarding, especially in deep, fresh, powder, delivers a sensation that is about as close to pure harmony as any extreme sport offers. Anyone who has experienced snowboarding has a clear understanding of why so many people, young and old, are taking to the mountains to try snowboarding.

IN SEARCH OF THE PERFECT LINE. BELOW: SNOWBOARDING HAS COME A LONG WAY SINCE THE ADVENT OF "THE SNURFER"; RIGHT: ON TOP OF THE WORLD... THE FEELING OF RIDING A SNOWBOARD CAN BE AWESOME.

ANOTHER EPIC POWDER DAY IN THE ALPS. RIGHT: RETO KESTENHOLZ WITH HIS TRADEMARK TAIL GRAB MANEUVER; BELOW: THERE'S NO LIMIT TO THE EXCITEMENT YOU CAN WHIP UP ON A SNOWBOARD.

Since the beginning, snowboarding has progressed from simple boards crudely constructed from wood, or molded plastic with metal fins attached—meant as a steering aid–to many of the high-tech wood and foam-core construction methods that ski manufacturers have been refining for years. The result is that today's snowboards are so stable and controllable that they are comfortable in every type of mountain terrain. Although skis offer better control on ice, the surface area of snowboards remains a bonus in deep snow because it allows them to float.

As for bindings, early designs used clumsy foot straps and some even had string attached to the nose for stability that offered little control. Today, binding systems fall into two basic categories: strap-in and step-in. Both systems use a soft boot that is more flexible and comfortable than the rigid ski boots used by pioneers. The difference lies in the placement of the binding. Strap-in bindings are attached to the board and use a ratchet system to tighten around the boot.

Step-in boots have all the support of the binding built into the boot and use a low-profile plate system on the board to step into. Step-in boots are less flexible but they do offer a hassle-free option that cuts out sitting down to strap in, instead you just step and go! Strap-in bindings are favored by purists for their flexibility, feel and the belief that the step-in is too close to the idea of ski bindings.

Snowboarding was reviled for years by skiers and the ski industry. Early on, most mountains would not allow snowboarders on their lift systems or their slopes. It was a conservative, high-income environment struggling to come to terms with the arrival of skateboarders and surfers in their towns and on their mountains. The ski industry was jealous of the gold rush that the snowboard industry was experiencing. But as with

anything, change takes time and despite a media frenzy over the conflict that even saw one British newspaper run the headline "Ban this killer craze," snowboarders and skiers in ski towns soon saw the benefits of each other. Tourists who had only read reports in the press of conflict and danger took longer to come round, but since skiing's style started to emulate snowboarding and the new sport has matured, the animosity has gone.

Snowboarding has brought a new look to the hills, with its "snow parks." These specially created areas have '"hits" (jumps) and obstacles like rails, picnic tables, and even buried cars and buses that the riders use like street obstacles on snow. Young skiers appreciated these additions and have gone on to create freestyle skiing as a result.

Snowboarders enjoy the parks because they offer a challenging alternative to some of the mundane terrain that skiers covet. The art of riding snow parks has become an important element of snowboard competition with the creation of "slope style," where riders use a line of obstacles in the park to make an overall impression.

Another major impact on snowboarding has been the recreation of skateboard half-pipes in snow. The half-pipe gives snowboarders an opportunity to rhythmically link aerial tricks as they descend the slope on which the half-pipe is constructed. They attract masses of riders to mountains that build them, and many riders prefer to hike the side of the pipe for each ride rather than use the available chair lift system. It makes pipe riding a very social affair as riders cheer each other on to bigger and better tricks.

Though discouraged by some snowboarding pioneers like Jake Burton Carpenter when they were introduced at the first World Snowboarding Championships in 1983, half-pipe freestyle competitions are major events in

117

most of today's competitions. Now they are just one facet of an incredibly wide array of freestyle genres available to snowboarders.

There is the aforementioned Slope style, quarter pipes, which are one transition facing uphill that riders can re-enter performing just one trick, but the most popular is Big Air. Jumps are constructed by Snowcats or piste machines, they have a kicker or take off ramp, a tabletop that is the flat section that must be cleared and then a landing slope.

These jumps have reached phenomenal proportions over the last five years and top-end riders can now clear jumps over 100ft (30m) in length travelling at over 40mph (65kph). Tricks performed on these kickers have gone from 360° rotations in the early Nineties to 1080° spins (three full rotations) and many riders can perform these going switch (backward)! One of the most recent areas of freestyle snowboarding to develop is Jibbing. It originated in areas of America where there is snow but very few hills.

Jibbing is using any man-made object, walls, dams and most commonly hand rails and ledges as playthings. It has developed to such an extent that it has become a major part of modern freestyle snowboarding.

Away from the freestyle domain, there are other disciplines. One of the most interesting is snowboarding's version of slalom. Originally a popular discipline for snowboarders using ski boots and narrow boards, slalom all but died out when people stopped using ski or hard boots. Instead snowboarders looked to motocross for inspiration, the result is "boardercross," a race down a motocross-style track with berms and jumps. The catch is that racers are not alone, there are between four and six other racers on the course at the same time making boardercross one of the most exciting disciplines for spectators in snowboarding.

MAJESTIC IN THE MOUNTAINS. FAR LEFT: HOURS OF PRACTICE PAY OFF WHEN YOU CAN DO A STUNT THIS WELL; LEFT: RETO KESTENHOLZ DEFYING GRAVITY; BELOW: BENI LENZIN CUTS ACROSS A VIRGIN SLOPE.

Away from the confines of the resorts the most dangerous events are undoubtedly "extreme" contests, generally held on slopes exceeding 40 degrees in pitch. Falling almost certainly means losing the event, but it can also end in serious injury. Given the steepness of the angle, a rider may actually accelerate during a fall, tumbling uncontrollably past rock outcrops and possibly over large cliffs.

Extreme riding requires the highest levels of technical and physical skill to get top to bottom, while seeking extra points for jumping over and off cliffs, cornices and windlips. The key to success lies in preparation, knowing not only the line that you need to take inside out, but also mountain knowledge that can help to avoid dangerous avalanche slopes and slough. Pronounced "sluff," this is the mini avalanche created when a rider turns on a steep slope, the top layer of snow is released by the turn and accelerates down the slope creating a mini snowslide. Slough can easily knock riders off their feet and carry them into danger.

Away from extreme competitions, there is also the opportunity for anyone to go heliboarding and this is the pinnacle of soul snowboarding. It offers snowboarders the chance to get taken by helicopter to the top of peaks that have untouched powder top to bottom, a guide is supplied to keep riders safe and offer advice. One day's heliboarding can cost as much as $500, so it is not cheap, but the sensation and memories it provides are something that will last a lifetime.

Snowboarding is one of the easiest extreme sports to learn whatever age you are and it takes place in some of the world's most beautiful natural environments.

It has something to offer everyone, whether you're young, old, aggressive, laid-back, serious or just a plain fun rider. Get out there before you regret it!

SNOWMOBILING

SNOWMOBILING IS NOT THE FIRST SPORT THAT YOU WOULD CALL EXTREME. A 2003 SURVEY FOUND THE AVERAGE AGE OF A SNOWMOBILER TO BE 41, HE—92 PER CENT ARE MEN—IS LIKELY TO BE MARRIED AND RIDES GROOMED TRAILS OR USES HIS SLED FOR ICE FISHING. SURELY THAT IS NOT AN EXTREME SPORT.

When you look at most people riding motorbikes on the road today they probably fit the same kind of description as the sled owners. But just as motor biking has freestyle motocross, so sledding has a dark side.

There is some controversy over who actually invented the snowmobile. In 1927 Carl J. Eliason got the first patent on a snow machine, unfortunately the specifics are too vague to give Eliason the credit.

The general view is that an inventive young engineer from Quebec going by the name of Joseph-Armand Bombardier was the first man to truly conquer snow travel with his 1930 prototype. Bombardier's tenacity was rewarded in 1958 when, after years of streamlining a 12-person passenger sled designed for postal services, police and military, he event-ually constructed a single man "Skidoo" that, with a reduced size and price, became a massive success in the harsh winters of America, Canada and Scandinavia.

Being used like winter cars, sleds soon found themselves being raced. In 1970 the U.S. Snowmobile Association was set up and they sanctioned over 250 races in their first winter. Like Formula One and Superbike racing, the Sleds became pocket rockets; bigger and bigger engines were getting mounted on snowmobiles while manufacturers tried to cope with the handling problems that were the side effect of all the extra power.

Frozen lakes provided a perfectly flat track for the races and it wasn't long before the U.S.S.A. had to ban people from using nitrous injections. For almost 20 years, the main focus of high-end snowmobiling lay in racing. That was all about to change.

Snowmobiles have always been used as a very practical way of getting around in snow. They take you many places other vehicles can not reach. It was no surprise that, when ski resorts in America and Canada started to get crowded in the early Nineties, expert snowboarders, skiers and film crews started to

move into the backcountry to build jumps and go freeriding.

The only ways to do this are by helicopter or by sled and if you've ever tried to hire a helicopter you'll know it's not cheap. Because of the incredible terrain accessed by the sleds, very often it was just as much fun to stay on the sled and do jumps, drop cliffs or find lines.

It didn't take long for everyone to realise the potential of the sleds in this environment and pretty soon a lot of the film crews were shooting as much sledding as skiing or snowboarding.

Soon there were snowmobile sections popping up in ski and snowboard films that were blowing people's minds. Bigger jumps and cliff drops than anyone had ever seen on skis or snowboards, let alone a snowmobile!

A normal snowmobile is not that different from a motorbike. Instead of a back wheel there is a giant rubber tread with paddles on it that dig into the snow and propel the sled forwards. You can get different-length paddles for different depths of snow. Two skis that steer, or are supposed to, replace the front wheel. Because the snow and ice are by nature slippery and unpredictable, steering, with the handlebars, is very hard. The throttle is a lever that you press with your thumb and acts as a good brake, but there is also a brake lever for the tread that sits on the handlebars.

On trails and groomed runs, snowmobiles are easy to control and great fun; the danger is when you take a sled in to deep powder snow.

Here it is much harder to control and very dangerous because the weight of the sled can easily set off avalanches if the snow is unstable. The key to snowmobiling is to never set off alone because the most common problem if you are out in deep snow is getting bogged, or sinking. If this happens, then you will need a good friend to haul your sled out.

The snowmobiles that professional skiers and snowboarders had been using to go into the backcountry were just off-the-shelf models like the ones described above. For this side of the sport to progress and become functional they needed specialist equipment.

They already had the powder treads with long paddles to give more power in deep snow, and wide skis on the front to help them float. But realistically this was like taking a Harley-Davidson to a motocross track. They needed better suspension. Sleds are now being made that can stand up to the beating that they are taking from jumps and drops. Windshields have now been all but removed after a couple of high-profile riders lost their teeth and one badly damaged his voice box.

While snowmobiling in the backcountry was just kicking off, the established world of

snowmobile racing was also responding to a new generation of riders who were looking for different challenges other than just flat out speed.

Taking a leaf out of the Motocross book, they created a Snocross series. The idea being that as well as flat out snowmobiling, speed racers would have to contend with man-made jumps and natural terrain. The sport is now a regular at the X Games and has educated a whole new generation to the capabilities of the snowmobile.

Snowmobiling may seem like an odd inclusion in an extreme sport book if you look at its heritage. But when you look at it from the point of view of the extreme generation (from the late Eighties through to now), the rate of its progression is phenomenal and it starts to make sense.

Jim Rippey, an enthusiastic sledder and very talented ex-professional snowboarder, backflipped a sled in 2000, the same year that Mike Metzger first backflipped a motocrosser! These kinds of feats of insanity are what are putting snowmobiling on the extreme map and will keep it there for some time to come.

SNOWMOBILES BEAT DOGSLEDS BY A MILE. LEFT: RUSH HOUR IN THE FROZEN WASTES; ABOVE: JOHN ELDRIDGE GETS AIR, VAIL PASS, COLORADO.

SPEED BIKING

TRAVELING DOWN A SNOW-COVERED 60-DEGREE SLOPE AT OVER 125 MPH ON SKIS IS EXTREME. BUT IT'S EASY COMPARED TO RIDING A MOUNTAIN BIKE DOWN THE SAME SLOPE AT THE SAME SPEED...

Over the past few years, downhill mountain bike racers have been pushing the limits of speed on specially outfitted mountain bikes, and have already broken the 125 mph (200kph) threshold. The bikes are fitted with special aerodynamic fairings and tires modified with large spikes to grip the snow and ice-covered surface as they accelerate to maximum velocity before racing through a speed-trap zone (a timed distance that determines the official speed established by the rider).

Speed bikes are wind tunnel-tested to improve aerodynamics before racing. Both rider and bike are outfitted to slice through the wind, and the resulting forms are thin and offer little resistance. The bikes are both suspended and unsuspended, and are raced in stock class and modified class. The suspension designs are stiffer than you'd expect in order to get off the shelf and give the rider a margin of error at speed that a rigid frame cannot, allowing for higher terminal velocities.

The current world record for speed biking is held by Frenchman Christian Taillefer, who was traveling at 132 mph (212 kph) at the Speed Ski Slope in Vars, France. Considering the world record for speed skiing is now 150+ mph (240kph) above that, we can expect to see far higher speeds as the technology of speed biking improves.

Speed biking is still relatively new as a sport, so it is safe to expect that the records established today will be broken and reestablished soon. Many world class mountain bike downhill racers and speed skiing racers crossing over to speed bikes will be working hard to determine the modifications needed for both equipment and training to make new records possible. The next few years should be very interesting.

CLOCKWISE (FROM TOP RIGHT): ERIC BARON (IN YELLOW) WHO HAS GONE OVER 120 MPH (195KPH); PEDALING DOWNHILL; ZOOM MAN; AERODYNAMIC MAN; MARKUS STOCKL IN LECH, AUSTRIA.

SPEED SKIING

IMAGINE SCREAMING DOWN A MOUNTAIN AT 150 MPH (240KPH) ON SKIS. CALIFORNIAN JEFF HAMILTON DID IT IN 1995, BECOMING THE FASTEST NON-MOTORIZED HUMAN ON THE PLANET.

Consider the forces at play when traveling at 150 mph. The skier is literally skiing faster than a sky diver in freefall. The skis are no longer even touching the ground at that speed. Instead they are riding on a cushion of air. Even the slightest error in judgment can be deadly.

What if a skier was to fall at speed? If they were fortunate enough not to break anything (legs, arms, etc.), it is unlikely they would avoid the residual burns that a high speed fall on snow leaves behind. The suits the skiers wear, while great at reducing drag, are not good at preventing tremendous heat build up from the friction of the snow during a fall. Former World Champion Franz Weber was reported to have spent well over a year healing from burns suffered during a high speed fall.

Clearly, if an athlete wishes to speed ski, he must be a top skier in tremendous physical condition. The forces on the skier's body during acceleration and at terminal velocity are awesome. Wind tunnel training is one key to finding a low-drag stance. It is expensive, but it allows top competitors to find a position through low-risk testing in a controlled environment. However, the fact remains that at some point, the skier will be asked to point their skis down a 2-mile (3.2km), 60-degree slope. If that isn't enough, at the bottom of that run, when their muscles are at their most taxed, they need to find the energy to stop.

Speed skiers employ many specialized pieces of equipment when performing their sport. First, their head protection is a strange looking helmet that is designed to fit flush with their upper body, minimizing any speed-robbing drag. Their poles are special aero-dynamically-shaped units, complementing their low-drag theme. Even the boots are modified for reduced drag, and their lower legs are smoothed by the addition of wing-like pants to further eliminate drag. Of course, all of these aero-additions don't mean squat if the skier can't hold a decent position during their run. That is where physical conditioning and endurance, preparation and mental toughness differentiate first from last.

Speed skiing competitions are held throughout Europe, but mostly in France, where they are major events. In North America, there are no areas that are accessible for speed skiing, and insurance and tort law problems make attempting events difficult, so the sport is widely overlooked. Speed skiing is rapidly gaining exposure and popularity globally, as the demand for more and varied extreme sport competitions grows.

SPEED KINGS. LEFT: SPEED SKIIERS' HELMETS CAN GIVE THEM THE APPEARANCE OF ALIENS FROM ANOTHER PLANET; BELOW: HARRY EGGER IN LECH, AUSTRIA.

STREET LUGE

THE ICE LUGE IS AN OLYMPIC SPORT WITH WHICH MOST OF THE WORLD IS FAMILIAR, AND WHICH FEW WOULD DENY IS EXTREME. ENTER THE PAVEMENT VERSION OF THE SPORT, STREET LUGE.

While street lugers don't have specially constructed tracks for their use, they do find steep and winding roads to roar down at speeds exceeding 70 mph (113kph). In the same way as ice luge is traditional sledding pushed to the limit, so street luge is an extension of skateboarding. In fact, skateboarders have traveled downhill on their boards at speed, both lying down on their backs like a street luge, on their stomachs, and standing up.

The street luge is an evolution of the traditional skateboard design. The wheels and trucks (the combined axle and steering mechanism) used by skateboards and street luges are pretty much the same, though luges tend to have wider axles than skateboards. The decks used by skateboarders (the board part of a skateboard) are replaced by stiffer metal and composite-frame systems that allow the street luge to be made longer and track better than a skateboard.

Decks on street luges must be stiffer because as the speed of the boards increase, the stresses placed on the decks increase to the point that a deck that is not stiff enough will begin to move, allowing the wheels to wobble. "High speed wobbles" are a big factor in limiting terminal velocity, not only in skateboards, but also inline skates, partly because the wheels do not have enough diameter or mass to stabilize themselves through centripetal force.

Once the luge deck is acceptable, the most important equipment is the wheels. At the speeds that street luges can travel, the bearings used to keep the wheels attached to the axles must work very hard, spinning almost as quickly as the wheels themselves. The slightest bit of friction within the bearing can "toast" a wheel, creating enough heat to melt the wheel where it contacts the bearing, and bringing a run to a quick stop. Therefore, street lugers pay particularly close attention to the details of cleaning and preparing their wheels before they start. Even so, dirt and dust particles can work their way into a bearing while the luger is moving, and the result can be the same.

Because lugers are traveling at high speeds on pavement, they must wear protect-ive gear. Most make use of the motorcycle leathers, which are generally expected to take all the abuse the luger's skin would suffer in the event of a fall. Leather gloves are also worn and a full-face helmet is necessary.

The final, and perhaps most important, piece of street luge equipment is the rider's footwear. The shoes are used as brakes, at which point they are exposed to the same kind of extreme heat as the wheels and bearings. Obviously, not just any shoe will work. Lugers use modified sneakers or boots to stop themselves. Typically, a section is removed from an automobile tire and fixed to the shoes' soles, giving them grippy rubber capable of stopping a car without melting, never mind a luge.

Street luging got its unofficial start in the foothills of Southern California, when groups of riders first began flying down the steep, smooth, and winding roads for thrills. Street luging is still relatively new, and so we can expect a variety of improvements in technology as the sport develops. Who knows, some day maybe we'll even see specialty tracks like the ones used in ice luge.

LEATHER SUITS, GLOVES AND SPECIALLY MODIFIED SHOES ARE PREQUISITES FOR STREET LUGERS. BELOW: TOOLS OF THE TRADE; RIGHT: FEET FIRST BURST—ON THE ROAD TO LOS ANGELES.

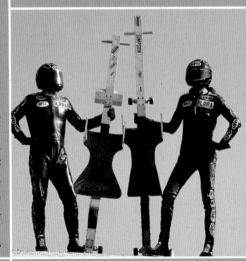

WATER SPORTS

WATER NOURISHES, AND IT CAN ALSO BRING DEATH. WE ARE NOT NATURALLY BUILT TO SURVIVE IN IT, BUT WE ARE DRAWN TO ITS MANY POSSIBILITIES FOR EXTREME SPORTS.

Water. Ninety per cent of our bodies are made of it. Two-thirds of the planet is covered by it. It is the most inhospitable of the earth's elements for human survival, yet without it, life would cease. If indeed all life began in the water, as modern theories of evolution suggest, perhaps this explains why we are so attracted to it, and why being in or near it fosters a sense of synergy. It welcomes us through some ethereal sense of belonging, and we respond by seeking to find any way we can to have fun in and on it. For as long as there has been human life, there have been opportunities for sport in the water.

For centuries stories have been told about the terrible demise of sailors eaten by mammoth sea creatures. A legacy of artwork depicting scenes of horror, with monsters eating entire ships full of people, speaks volumes about how far from fearful superstition we have come. Many of the mysteries surrounding the oceans and lakes covering the planet have long been solved.

Sailboats are now built to be raced on courses that circumnavigate the globe. Consider that it was only 500 years ago that Columbus successfully crossed the Atlantic and found the New World, a trip that is now made daily in only hours by jet.

Yet the oceans still have many dangers, both seen and unseen. Rocks or reefs clearly visible at a low tide might lie just beneath the water's surface at high tide. Being aware of them by seeing and understanding the clues they leave on the water's surface when they are submerged is a valuable skill, whether surfing or sailing. Being able to avoid them, especially at speed, can mean the difference between life and death.

Beneath the surface, the risks are far greater, ranging from being attacked by aggressive or hungry sea dwellers to falling

CLOCKWISE (FROM NEAR RIGHT): ORLANDO DUQUE CLIFF DIVING AT LANAI, HAWAII; GRANT BAKER CHASING THE REDBULL BIG WAVE, NEAR CAPE TOWN; SOLO FREE DIVING; BAREFOOT WATER SKIING.

prey to any one of several things that go wrong when using a breathing apparatus. Human beings were not meant to survive under water, and by exploring its depths we leave ourselves exposed and vulnerable.

Rivers hold many of the same hidden dangers, yet they occur with such frequency that avoiding them is actually the sport. It is the rocks and boulders that give whitewater its name, not just the speed at which the water travels, and athletes wishing to test their abilities must be able to react quickly and decisively if they are to survive life-threatening situations.

When struck at speed, water takes on properties that are closer to cement than any liquid. The water's surface texture is ever-changing, creating opportunities for jumping, often at inappropriate times. Some sources for jumping are also sources of propulsion; such is the case with waves for boardsailers and surfers, who view surf very differently.

How each athlete views water is as different as the sports they pursue. Large swells and waves make for great surfing, but without breeze, poor boardsailing. A strong breeze makes for great boardsailing, but strong winds can ruin an incredible surf day by changing the waves from clean and smooth to messy and chopped up.

What makes these water sports extreme is that each was created by redefining the limits of what was possible in terms of human and technological performance on and under the water. Anyone wishing to know how long a swimmer can stay submerged or how far a swimmer can travel under their own power can look to these sports for answers. That is because someone made it their task and their passion to find out for themselves what they were capable of doing in or on water.

CLOCKWISE (FROM TOP RIGHT): WAVESAILING IN THE CANARY ISLANDS; POWERBOATING; VISSER 'JIMBO' JAMES HANGS ON TO HIS JET SKI IN MAUI, HAWAII; YACHTING ON THE OPEN OCEAN; SCUBA DIVING.

BAREFOOT WATER SKIING

SPORTS ARE ABOUT COMPETITION AS WELL AS CONTACT. SPORTS WHICH INVOLVE THE THRILL OF SPEED INVARIABLY REQUIRE SPECIALIZED EQUIPMENT, BUT THE NEARER THE ELEMENTS YOU GET, THE MORE INTENSE THE EXPERIENCE. SO FOR WATER SKIIERS, WHAT COULD MAKE MORE SENSE THAN DISPENSING WITH SKIS?

Barefoot water skiing began in Winter Haven, Florida in 1947. Water skiing pioneer Chuck Sligh theorized that water skiing without skis might be possible if the ski boat went fast enough. A 17-year-old boy named AG Hancock proved him right, becoming the first water skier to drop a ski and continue barefoot successfully. Hancock left on a family vacation before he could show the trick to Cypress Garden's Dick Pope Sr. A few days later, Pope's son Dick Jr. successfully dropped a ski and got all the glory—photographs, newspaper stories, newsreels, the works. Barefoot skiers soon adapted many of the freestyle moves of traditional waterskiers. Spins, backward maneuvers, body drags, and other tricks made barefooting an exciting new discipline. Due to the speeds required to barefoot, the tricks are especially difficult, and dangerous, since the water becomes very hard in a high-speed impact.

Barefoot water skiing quickly became a cult sport, especially in Australia. Barefoot clubs and competitions took place throughout the Sixties without too many people outside of the sport taking notice. Sometime around 1967 the Australians began experimenting with barefoot jumping. No one knows who the first barefoot jumper was, but he set in motion a chain of events that eventually brought his sport some long-overdue attention.

In 1973, the Australians introduced the Americans to barefoot jumping at the International Championships, held at Cypress Gardens. It wasn't until 1978 that jumping was included as an event at the first U.S. Barefoot Nationals. That same year Greg Rees of Australia set the first official world record at 44 feet (13.41m).

The techniques used at this time were foot-to-foot, where the jumper used his feet for both the take-off and the landing, and something called bum jumping. Bum jumpers went up and off the ramp on their buttocks and then tried to land on their feet, a technique that resulted in longer jumps, but was uncontrollable.

Even this spectacle wasn't enough to garner a lot of mainstream attention. That changed in 1989 when U.S. jumper Mike Seipel accidentally invented the inverted style of jumping while training in Florida. The first time it happened Seipel says the thought that occurred to him was "I'm going to kill myself," so he let go of the handle and splashed in. Then he realized that he had flown farther, so he tried it again, sticking the landing on his third try.

In the inverted style, the jumper pushes forward at the top of the ramp and lets the handle out. This puts the jumper horizontal to the water, flying most of the distance of the jump in that position, then swinging his body back down for a landing, hopefully on his feet and buttocks. The first time Seipel tried it in competition he broke the world record, flying 72.5 feet (22.10m).

The sport immediately exploded. Jumpers who were initially skeptical of the new technique quickly learned it, and average jumps went from 40–50 feet up to 60–70 feet. The International World Water Ski Federation world barefoot jump record was set by David Small of Great Britain in February 2004 at 89.05 feet (27.4m), and the 100 foot mark is expected to fall soon.

BAREFOOT IN THE WATERPARK. (CLOCKWISE FROM TOP RIGHT): TAKE OFF; MARC ALEXANDER OF FRANCE; MIKE SEIPEL AND HIS UNUSUAL JUMP STYLE.

CLIFF DIVING

IT IS VERY DIFFICULT TO PINPOINT THE EXACT TIME OR PLACE WHEN HUMANS, IN THEIR WISDOM, DECIDED TO CHALLENGE THEIR LIMITS AND THROW THEMSELVES INTO THE WATER FROM VERY HIGH CLIFFS.

The challenge of overcoming your fear, the physical limitations of the human body, and the adrenaline reward for believing in yourself are the factors that have seen millions of people throughout the ages hurling themselves from rocks and cliffs just for the fun of it.

Cliff diving is without question the most accessible extreme sport on the planet. Although Polynesians and other island-dwelling races had probably been happily leaping off rocks for millennia, they unfortunately didn't make any record of it, which means the first documented evidence of cliff divers belongs to the Europeans. The earliest proof of cliff diving appeared in the Mediterranean—a two-and-a-half-thousand-year-old tomb in Naples has etchings of a man diving from a rock or cliff, and historians believe it was one of the disciplines in the ancient Greek games.

Although many small communities with the right facilities—a high ledge above some deep water—would practice cliff diving as a right of passage for young men, the rugged art of cliff diving lost favor in the civilized world when "fancy diving" was invented in the seventeenth century. Gymnasts from Sweden and Germany began practicing and it became a popular spectator sport, attracting large crowds. The sport progressed and was eventually accepted into the Olympics in 1904 still under the title fancy diving.

As competition diving became more popular and the parameters of competition were set at a 3-meter springboard and a 10-meter solid board, so divers looked to take their skills outside the confines of the arena. This was the point when the sport of cliff diving as we know it today was born. Accomplished gymnasts took their skills out of the sterile environs of a swimming pool and onto the dangerous and unpredictable coastlines of the world.

ONLY THE BRAVEST ATTEMPT CLIFF DIVING. LEFT: IF YOU HIT ANY SURFACE AT 70MPH IT FEELS LIKE CONCRETE—EVEN WATER. HERE A MEXICAN DIVER PLUNGES HEAD FIRST INTO THE SEA IN ACAPULCO.

Acapulco in Mexico is the place that springs to mind when most people think of famous cliff diving spots. La Quebrada, as the cliffs are called, is a dramatic rock formation on Acapulco's western coast and the ledges used by the divers tower between 55 and 70ft (17–22m). But it is not the height of the ledges that has led to La Quebrada being known as the most treacherous dive on the high diving circuit—most of the competitions are held off ledges in the 75–78ft (25–26m) range. Instead it is the depth of the water that keeps divers on their toes. At a mere eight feet deep in places, participants cannot afford to make a single mistake.

Although there is no recognised tour for high diving, the separate events around the world have pooled their expertise for the betterment of the sport. Events now take place all over the world, in Monaco, the Amalfi coastline in Southern Italy, the lakes of Switzerland and Austria, Acapulco in Mexico and Hawaii.

As most of the divers are trained Olympic athletes looking for challenges outside their regular regime, competition is fierce. But despite the high-profile daredevil image, there is no pot of gold waiting for those taking part.

Because of the highly skilled nature of the sport and the risk of career-threatening injuries or even death, there are only a handful of cliff divers on earth capable of attempting the most difficult jumps. Injuries sustained can be horrific for even the smallest of mistakes. Once a diver has jumped, he will accelerate up to around 70mph (113kph) in just three seconds, coming to a dead stop in the space of 12ft (four metres).

If you hit any surface at 70mph, it will feel like concrete as any cliff diver can tell you. If the arms aren't pressed hard enough against the body, then they will get pulled up to where collar bones break or shoulders end up dislocating. If your fingers are sticking out as you enter the water, then they will snap like match sticks; if you are tilting forwards then the force of the impact on your chest will push

all of the air out of your lungs and you will sink like a stone. Imagine what happens when your chin sticks out! The list of potential dangers goes on, but one of the most interesting and terrifying is the concept of an aftershock.

When divers break the surface of the water, their bodies must be locked rigid to prevent anything from breaking under the stress of impact, then as divers enter the water they create a pocket of air, which, as they slow down is pushed back to the surface. This means that the water crashes back into the diver for a second time, only this time it's with the phenomenal force of the sea itself. Any diver that doesn't brace himself, or herself, for a massive secondary impact can find themselves with serious internal injuries like crushed ribs or a broken pelvis.

Cliff diving is easily the cheapest extreme sport to try, but it is also the most dangerous. If you look at the photos here it is the height of the cliff and the risk that you notice first, but then the almost unbelievable grace and style of the diver shines through. Cliff diving is a truly incredible feat of human achievement.

139

FREEDIVING

THERE IS A SPECIAL BREED OF DIVER WHO CAN GO DEEPER THAN MOST, WITHOUT AIR TANKS. THESE FREEDIVERS HAVE PUSHED THE LIMITS OF UNASSISTED BREATHING DIVES TO BELOW 400 FEET.

To freedive to depths of even 50 feet (15m) is an unsettling prospect for all but the strongest swimmers. To dive much deeper requires holding a breath for minutes. In fact, the world's best freedivers hold their breath for periods that rival many marine mammals.

There are three categories of freediving for depth. The first there is "fixed weight" or "fixed volume" diving. Divers in this discipline swim down as deep as they can under their own power, and resurface the same way.

The main drawback to this method is that it means using up valuable air in the descent, at the same time limiting the speed at which divers can get deep, and therefore also the depths attainable.

The current record is over 240 feet (73m), and was set by Frenchman Eric Charrier in 1995. Fixed weight divers use high-technology composite swim fins to aid them in going down and coming up.

The second is "variable weight" freediving, in which ballast is used to aid divers descend; up to one-third of body weight is considered legal. Variable weight divers can get down faster and with less effort than fixed weight divers, yet they must still swim back to the surface under their own power. Again the use of special fins is a requirement.

The third is called "absolute" diving, which allows unlimited ballast in the descent, with rates reaching 12–15 feet per second (3.6–4.6m). To return to the surface, the diver grabs a lifting aid, such as an inflatable bag. Francisco "Pipin" Ferraras from Cuba used a weighted sled for his world record dive into Los Cabos Bay, Mexico, in 2003. He plunted to 552.5 feet (170m) in a dive lasting 2mins 40 secs until his air tanks inflated.

How divers like Ferraras and Umberto Pelizarri reach these depths is by learning to control their body's ability to sustain them between breaths. But regardless of how it is done, prolonged periods between breaths can result in latent hypoxia, or "shallow water blackout." Ironically, shallow water blackout occurs usually just below the surface and the diver can drown if unassisted. Many use specialized advanced breathing methods, like the Tai'Chi yoga breathing technique.

These methods aid the divers in controlling and even reducing the rate of their metabolism, thus decreasing the need for oxygen. Another—though less zen-related method—is to hyperventilate. This involves prolonged deep breathing before the dive, which increases the ratio of oxygen in the lungs and effectively "tricks" the body into lowering its need to breathe so frequently. This is not as effective as meditation.

Freedivers must economize their movement in order to maximize their time underwater. Each move requires oxygen, and there is clearly a limited supply. Good divers don't rush the process and, as a result, can remain under water for longer periods.

Freediving embodies the extreme athlete's quest for inner control and improved performance in sports. Without question, a failed attempt can end in death and, as with so many other extreme sports, athletes must be fully prepared both mentally and physically if they are to succeed.

THE BIG BLUE. BELOW: UMBERTO PELIZARRI EXPERIENCES PRESSURE 16 TIMES GREATER THAN NORMAL DURING HIS DIVES; RIGHT: A "NO LIMITS" DIVE ON THE TURKS AND CAICOS ISLANDS.

JET SKIING

IN 1965 A CALIFORNIAN BANKER WITH A PASSION FOR MOTORCYCLES CONCEIVED AN AQUATIC VEHICLE WHICH WOULD BECOME KNOWN WORLDWIDE AS THE JET SKI. AN EXTREME SPORT WAS BORN...

Clayton Jacobson enjoyed building racing motorcycles in his spare time. He loved going fast on motorcycles—but crashing on hard pavement was not what he considered to be their appeal. The concept of the Jet Ski was born from Jacobson's theory that a motorcycle for the water would be just as fun to ride as the ones he enjoyed building, but without the pain of a hard landing if you fell off. Mr. Jacobson would be correct.

Jacobson built a few prototypes from his designs, and after being issued a patent in 1969, licensed his design to Ski-Doo manufacturer Bombardier. Bombardier ran into several problems and halted development a

year later. Their license to use the design expired in 1971, and within months Jacobson signed a deal with Kawasaki to use his design. In 1973 Kawasaki introduced the Jet Ski, the first stand-up personal watercraft. Clayton Jacobson's concept soon became one of the most successful boat designs in history.

What made the Jet Ski possible was that Jacobson utilized a jet water-pump system rather then the Sixties state-of-the-art inboard or outboard motor propulsion systems. These motors utilize an external propeller to provide thrust. The Jet Ski design uses an internal water-jet motor for thrust. The motor draws water into itself and shoots a stream out again to generate

thrust, without exposing potentially hazardous blades that can injure a rider. Current engines deliver in excess of 85 horsepower and can push the Jet Ski to speeds exceeding 50 mph (80kph).

The correct term for the jet-driven craft currently available is "personal watercraft." Because the sit-down design is far less physically demanding than the stand-up Jet Ski, they have far broader consumer appeal, and now make up over 95 per cent of the personal watercraft market.

Both stand-up and sit-down designs offer a sense of freedom and performance that is unrivaled by other small motorized boats. They allow riders to use their bodies to enhance the watercraft's performance. Much like the motorcycles they were intended to replicate, personal watercraft give riders a wind-and-water-in-the-face sensation that is addictive to say the least.

Competitive events are held internationally, and include closed-course racing and freestyle riding. The freestyle events are meant to showcase each rider's skills by requiring them to execute a series of difficult and creative maneuvers within a predetermined time period, generally two minutes. Each rider is scored by a panel of seven judges, issuing points from 1–10. The rider with the highest score wins. Riders execute a range of tricks,

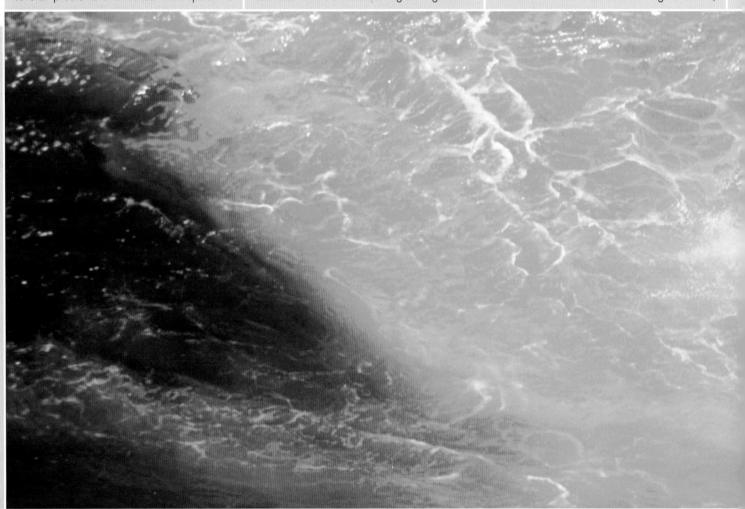

including submerging their watercraft and shooting it up out of the water, as well as jumps and spins requiring strength and agility.

The closed-course races require groups of riders to race each other around a set of buoys, with the winner determined at the finish line. The closed courses include a series of right- and left-hand turns, requiring riders to be strong all-around drivers. These races take place as a series of elimination heats. The top finishers advance to the next race until a group reaches the final heat. The finishing positions in the final heat determine the overall winners.

Events are broken down into three classes. The first is the Runabout Division, consisting of sit-down personal watercraft designed to seat one or more. The second is the Sport Division, which uses lighter, higher-performance versions of sit-down watercraft. The third is the Ski Division, which comprises stand-up designs for one rider.

In many ways personal watercraft have redefined water activities and their costs. These vehicles average around $8,550 (£5,700), bringing a new affordability to performance watercraft. This is especially in-expensive when

HOLD ON TO YOUR HATS. RIGHT: JET SKI RACING COMPETITION EVENTS INCLUDE THE SKI DIVISION FOR A SINGLE STAND-UP RIDER; BELOW: JET SKIING ON THE LEGENDARY JAWS WAVES OF HAWAII.

you consider that many outboard motors of similar horsepower cost around the same price without the boat attached. Because they were designed to be fallen from, each personal watercraft has one or two safety devices. First is an automatic steering mechanism to direct the watercraft in circles after a rider has fallen off. Second is a cord that is attached to the driver and the ignition system. If the rider falls off, the engine turns off and the watercraft awaits the swimming driver.

Even these safety devices cannot replace commonsense. All personal watercraft riders should wear flotation devices, and a helmet is a good idea too, when extreme riding. Many drivers like to travel at high speed close to other riders, then spin around fast. Top experts may be capable of doing this with reasonable control, but novices should stay away from other watercraft, especially other novices. The craft are heavy at speed, and collisions can have terrible consequences.

Jet-drive watercraft are used for a range of sports today, including waterskiing, wakeboarding, and—most dramatically—tow-in surfing, a sport that started in the massive waves off Maui, Hawaii, where personal watercraft drivers can quickly tow surfers on narrow high-performance surfboards out to big waves that would be unsurfable if the surfers weren't moving before the wave caught them.

The popularity of personal watercraft is underscored by the frequency with which they are visible at beaches and on waterways around the world.

There is not a beach resort anywhere that doesn't have at least one available for rent. The reason seems obvious, personal watercraft allow boaters and non-boaters the opportunity to get out on the water and experience a sense of freedom that was previously only reserved for motorcyclists.

ALL HANDS ON DECK. LEFT: THE RUNABOUT DIVISION IS A JET SKIING EVENT FOR CRAFT WITH MORE THAN ONE RIDER; BELOW: THE SPORT DIVISION IS FOR LIGHTER, HIGHER-PERFORMANCE CRAFT.

OPEN WATER SWIMMING

SWIMMING LONG DISTANCES FOR SPORT IS A CHALLENGE THAT ONLY THE FITTEST AND MOST DETERMINED EXTREME ATHLETES PURSUE. ITS ROOTS CAN BE TRACED BACK TO AS LONG AGO AS 1875 WHEN CAPTAIN MATTHEW WEBB CONQUERED ALL ODDS AND BECAME THE FIRST SWIMMER TO CROSS THE ENGLISH CHANNEL.

Open water is the appropriate term, since races and crossings are never held in a pool, as that would be lacking in the essential element—danger. Open water swimming races are held globally, and were included in many of the early Olympic Games. Course lengths are usually 5, 10, 15, or 25 kilometers (3–15.5 miles) and require several hours to complete. The courses are set between two points on any large body of water.

Open water swimming may seem like an individual achievement, however open water swimmers always work with a coach, who travels nearby in a boat. The coach's job is to monitor the swimmer's performance, give feedback, and insure the swimmer doesn't get into danger while competing. The coach's boat also doubles as a rescue craft.

Swimmers can come across natural hazards during the course of an event, ranging from life-threatening sea creatures to debris and rough water. The coach endeavors to guide the swimmer around hazards. A common hazard is jellyfish. The threat of being stung is ever present, and given that most stings occur directly on the face and neck, a most unpleasant event. Another is sharks.

When a shark is sighted, swimmers naturally react by swimming faster out of added adrenaline. Attacks, however, are not common, and it is the coach's duty to assess any shark presence for signs of aggression.

Swimmers are not allowed to wear any kind of wetsuit, so hypothermia is a key concern during any event. Again, it is the duty of the coach to determine whether the swimmer is becoming hypothermic, and if so to encourage them to work harder to boost their body temperature. If the swimmer is unable to combat hypothermia, it is the coach's job to get them out of the water and retire from the race, a task that is not always as easy as it sounds.

Open water swimmers must be in tremendous physical condition to deal with the demands these events put upon them. Athletes must train constantly, with little opportunity for diversity. The stamina and pain thresholds for each athlete must be at maximum for them to be competitive. Swimmers must maintain effort through rough and cold water, persevere in difficult currents, tidal surges, and wind-driven waves. Any one of these can cause the contestant to lose way, even lose some of the distance they've worked so hard to cover.

Open water swimming is an extreme endurance event in which only the most determined succeed.

IN THE SWIM. CLOCKWISE (FROM TOP LEFT): SPAIN'S DAVID MECA PLUS DRINK; EDITH VAN DIJK CUTS THROUGH THE WATER; OPEN WATER RACE IN VANCOUVER, BRITISH COLUMBIA, CANADA.

POWERBOAT RACING

NOT VERY LONG AGO, MOTORIZED BOATS CAPABLE OF 30–40 MPH (48–64KPH) WERE CONSIDERED FAST. NOW THE TECHNOLOGY OF BOAT CONSTRUCTION PLUS THE HORSEPOWER AVAILABLE TO MODERN ENGINES HAS GIVEN US POWER BOATS ABLE TO EXCEED 140 MPH (225KPH).

The driving force in the quest for powerboat speed has been racing. Since the first powerboat sped across the English Channel in 1903, the quest for speed has pushed powerboat technology forward tremendously. That sprint from Calais, France to Dover, England took place on a 39-foot (12m) hull powered by a 75 horse power Daimler engine. Pleasure boaters can use that kind of power plant on one of many small, light fiberglass boats commercially available without even blinking. Open-class racing boats today boast horse power ratings of over 1000.

Powerboats use two different types of engine. The first and original power plant is the "inboard" engine. Inboards are placed in the middle of the hull and turn a propeller via a driveshaft that passes through the hull toward the stern of the boat. Still widely used in racing, inboards offer a low center of gravity which improves the boat's stability.

Second is the "outboard." Outboards are essentially lightweight units clamped to the transom (the vertical plane at the stern). Outboards are commonly used to power smaller racing hulls and pleasure boats, and because they are compact and outside the hull, their use creates more room for gear and occupants. The drawback is the height of the weight placement of the motor, and the

placement of the weight so far back in the hull. This makes outboard-powered hulls less stable than inboard-powered, especially when the motors are proportionately large compared to the boat.

Racing boats utilize three distinct hull designs. First is the "Deep V" originated by U.S. designer Dick Bertram. The hull has a V-shape running through the hull's center from the bow (front) to the stern (rear). The angle of the V is sharp at the bow and gradually tapers to a flatter angle at the stern. A series of "steps" runs the length of the hull, and provides lift and stability. Bertram's Deep V changed the powerboat world virtually

overnight after winning the 1960 Miami Nassau Race in a record eight hours. The design, with its sharp angles forward and stepped hull, allowed his boat to travel faster in rougher conditions than the flatter, unstepped hulls of the period. Today, almost every modern V-hull utilizes Bertram's design.

Second is a catamaran design consisting of two very sharp V-hulls mounted side by side. Modern racing "cats" are more efficient and therefore require less horsepower than the single V-hull design. Where races allow both V- and cat-hulls to compete, more powerful engines are usually allowed in the V-hull designs to offset the cats' advantage in efficiency.

Third is the hydrofoil design, which uses a wide, flat hull and two shallow asymmetrical cat-style hulls mounted forward and outside of the flat central hull. Used only in flat-water areas, these boats use tremendous horsepower to accelerate out of the turns in what are usually oval courses. In the turns, they rely on fins mounted to their hulls to keep them from sliding sideways. These boats look more like aeroplanes than powerboats.

PEDAL TO THE METAL. BELOW: HOT CATAMARAN; FROM TOP RIGHT: HYDROFOILS HAVE EXTRA ACCELERATION; OVERTAKING ON THE LEFT; CAT-HULL POWERBOATS SKIM ACROSS THE WATER.

There are many different types of powerboat racing around the world. The following is a list of the seven most commonly found internationally:

- CLASS A – the entry level in offshore racing, boats must be V-hulled of 24–30 feet (7.3–9m), similar to those available at dealers, and are limited to dual-outboard or single-inboard engine power capable of 70–80 mph (113–130kph)
- CLASS B – V-hull boats 30–38 feet (9–11.5m) powered by two inboard engines, with a speed range of 80–100 mph (130–160kph)
- CLASS C – catamarans of 28–30 feet (8.5–9m) powered by two outboard engines capable of 100–110 mph (160–177kph)—consistently one of the most evenly matched classes
- CLASS P – "pro stock" racers, all cat designs of 30–38 feet (9–11.5m), with three outboard engines and top speeds averaging 100–115 mph
- CLASS M – "Modified" class hulls can be either cat or V design. V-hulls are allowed to carry more horsepower due to the efficiency advantage cat hulls have
- OPEN CLASS – hulls generally in excess of 35 feet (11m), with engines of 1,000 horsepower and greater, capable of around 135 mph (217kph)—the premier class of offshore racing
- UNLIMITED CLASS – unlimited hydrofoils—the fastest of powerboat racers, but their designs confine them to the calm waters of lakes and protected shore regions—are powered by inboards, outboards, and even jet engines capable of speeds exceeding 150 mph (240kph).

Offshore racing boats have a crew of two or three in order to effectively manage their hulls at speed. The driver must concentrate solely on steering and keeping the boat under control, while an additional crew member controls the throttle and navigates. A third may be onboard as navigator for the larger Open Class boats. Powerboats are prone to violent crashes, largely thanks to inconsistent water surfaces. Even small waves hitting the hull in an odd or unexpected way are capable of sending boats flying out of the water where they become like uncontrollable aircraft. Sometimes landings can be smooth, but backward flips and hard impacts are more likely. And because of the excessive speeds, the results can be deadly—at 100+ mph, water behaves like cement.

Modern racing boats are designed to self-destruct in the event of a crash in order to lessen the impact. Impact zones and energy-absorbing construction techniques are doing much to reduce the frequency of serious driver injuries. Because the boats are prone to accidents, many occupants use a five-point harness system for protection. But some crews prefer not using safety harnesses in order to be thrown clear of the hull if they do crash—the greatest fear is being held underwater and drowned in the event of an accident.

Unlike most extreme sports, powerboat racing is expensive, and so crews rely on sponsors to buy signage on their hulls in order to offset the financial burden. Powerboats require a lot of time in testing designs and engines to insure competitiveness, further adding to the cost of racing. Many top teams spend well in excess of $1.5 million (£1 million) annually to be competitive and race.

The nature of powerboat racing requires participants to constantly test and reevaluate current technologies. As these technologies are advanced, it is conceivable that something will happen to enhance the safety of racing. However, it is unlikely that traveling at speed on the water will ever be considered a thrill that anyone but an extreme enthusiast will enjoy.

CAREFUL HOW YOU GO. BELOW: OUTBOARD POWER BOAT RACES ARE THE MOST POPULAR; RIGHT: POWER BOATS ARE PRONE TO VIOLENT CRASHES, MOSTLY DUE TO UNEVEN WATER SURFACES.

ROUND THE WORLD YACHT RACING

THE TROPHÉE JULES VERNE IS A CREWED, NON-STOP RACE AROUND THE WORLD INSPIRED BY THE EXPLOITS OF PHILEAS FOGG IN VERNE'S NOVEL *AROUND THE WORLD IN 80 DAYS*.

The race for the Trophée Jules Verne began in the fall of 1993, when a French and a New Zealand boat passed an imaginary line stretching across the western approaches to the English Channel, which later marked the finish line. The two multihulls streaked down the Atlantic Ocean until, somewhere south of Cape Town, South Africa, the New Zealand entry hit a submerged object. One of its hulls damaged, the crew were forced to life-saving measures to keep the catamaran afloat. They eventually made port under their own power, to return a year later and play an important role in the development of this young race.

As the New Zealanders limped toward South Africa, the Frenchmen pressed on. A six-man crew led by world record-holder Bruno Peyron, and including American specialist Cam Lewis, were sailing a huge and powerful catamaran, *Commodore Explorer*. The craft measured 88 feet (27m).

Catamarans are among the fastest type of sailboat in the world. With their hulls spread so far apart and the main power unit, the mast and mainsail, placed in between those hulls, catamarans can leverage the wind, sailing

A LIFE ON THE OCEAN WAVE. LEFT: *LA POSTE*,
AN ENTRY IN THE WHITBREAD RACE, 1993–94;
BELOW: THE YACHT *PELAGIC* **BRAVES ANTARCTICA;**
FLEURY MICHON X **OUT ON THE OPEN OCEAN.**

nearly twice as fast as the windspeed in a variety of wind and sea conditions.

Harnessing and controlling speed, both windspeed and boatspeed, is a problem with multihulls, and is most problematic in the winds and waves of the Southern Ocean. With no land mass to slow the prevailing currents, the Southern Ocean, generally considered the body of water below latitude 50°S, is the most treacherous stretch of sea on the planet. Wave heights topping 50 feet (15m) and windspeeds in excess of 75 mph (120 kph) can develop instantly, bringing with them hail, sleet, or blinding snowstorms.

With no visibility, radar is heavily relied on to see icebergs that could sink a boat with just a glancing blow. Most bergs are the size of a New York City street block, so the electronic seeing eye usually picks them up easily. Not so visible, however, are "growlers," large chunks of ice that break off the bergs. Growlers are typically half-submerged and commonly jut out underwater. They are so sharp that they can easily puncture the composite hulls of today's ocean racing sailboats.

The Frenchmen survived collisions with whales, they survived hurricanes, they survived hull damage, they survived hitting submerged logs, and they rewarded themselves by becoming the first sailing vessel to circumnavigate the globe by water in less

than 80 days. They covered 27,372 miles (44,041km) in 79 days, 6 hours, 15 minutes and 56 seconds, a total of 1,902 consecutive hours at sea.

Their record would stand for only a year, though. The New Zealanders returned and crushed *Commodore Explorer*'s record. Skippers Peter Blake, winner of the Whitbread Round the World Race, and Robin Knox-Johnston, the first man to singlehandedly circumnavigate the globe non-stop, created a team full of experience and commonsense.

They used the experience gained in their previous, aborted attempt to modify their catamaran. They increased its overall length to 92 feet (28m), modified the hull shape, and changed the rig configuration. The new and improved craft then took them and a crew of five around the world in a record time of 74 days, 22 hours, 17 minutes and 22 seconds.

But that record has since been obliterated. In 2002, Peyron spent 64 days, 8 hours, 37 minutes and 24 seconds at sea, captaining *Orange* on its voyage. Then, at 2.45 pm GMT on 5 April 2004, the intrepid American adventurer Steve Fossett—who in 2002 became the first man to circumnavigate the world in a balloon—completed the around the world race in just 58 days, 9 hours 32 minutes and 45 seconds. His maxi-catamaran *Cheyenne* had an international crew of 12.

THE WHITBREAD/ VOLVO OCEAN RACE

Offshore sailboat racing has two distinct disciplines. At one end of the spectrum is singlehanded sailing, where a solitary skipper puts his sailing knowledge, navigational expertise, will—even his life—on the line. At the other is crewed sailing, where crews between 12–20 sailors, specializing in particular tasks, rely upon one another as a team in the quest for victory.

Among the greatest races in the world in crewed racing is the Whitbread Round the World Race. Dubbed the "ultimate ocean race," it was the first of its kind, with origins dating back to 1973.

Four years earlier, in 1969, Englishman Robin Knox-Johnston had won the Golden Globe Race, and was the first to singlehandedly circumnavigate the globe non-stop. He was one of eight to start the challenge sponsored by London newspaper *The Sunday Times*, but the only sailor to finish. The event was considered more a challenge than a race because competitors were allowed to begin their voyage at any time between June and October of 1968.

Knox-Johnston's accomplishment started a frenzy of activity to organize the first official round the world race for fully crewed sailboats. Watching with keen interest were the British navy and army, who were in the process of obtaining several 55-foot (17m) boats for adventure training. When rivals couldn't get a race organized by April 1972, the British navy forged ahead with the Whitbread, and in September 1973 a legend was born. The first competition was historic for many reasons: it was the first, crewed, circum-navigational race of its kind; it was the first race of its kind to send crews into the treacherous waters known as the Roaring Forties and Screaming Fifties—the Southern Ocean; and it resulted in the fastest, crewed circumnavigation of its time.

The race proved even more challenging than the competitors had imagined. Leg two of the four-legged course took the fleet of 17 entrants from Cape Town, South Africa, to Sydney, Australia; and leg three went from Sydney to Rio de Janeiro, Brazil. Not only were these extremely long distances to sail, but they covered the Southern Ocean, the great expanse of water separating the six inhabited continents from the seventh, Antarctica. Unimpeded by land, storm systems sweep across these deep southern latitudes, gaining so much force that they become life threatening.

Three lives were lost in the Southern Ocean, all the result of crew members falling overboard. One sailor was presumably unconscious when a sheet flung him over. Another was swept off the deck during a sail change, when a huge breaking wave hit the boat. The third man was lost as he went forward for a sail change, apparently lost his footing and fell overboard. Down below on the vessels, crews worked frantically to keep water out of the boats—an almost impossible task at latitude 60°S.

In 1998, the Whitbread Race evolved into the Volvo Ocean Race, a fully corporate, sponsored, and highly glamorous competition. Whereas the first race in 1973/74 was largely a corinthian effort, today some skippers can earn as much as $150,000 (£100,000) to lead a corporation's entry. There are more legs for the next race than there were in the original, nine as opposed to four, and the boats are drastically different.

Unlike the crews of the original Whitbread, their counterparts today are as much concerned with how to get water into the boat as they are with keeping it out. The introduction of water-ballast systems (very common among the singlehanded spectrum) is a feature on the new class of boats, 60-footers (18m) capable of reaching speeds nearly three times as great in the Southern Ocean as the 1973–74 pioneers were able to.

The Volvo Ocean Race incorporates a vast array of challenges ranging from surviving powerful storms, to exhaustion, and even continuing after crew deaths. The crews are aware that they too could be lost at sea, that their yachts may not return, and that—at the very least—they will be required to perform at their physical and mental peaks for months with only a few onshore breaks. This is team sailboat racing at its most extreme.

GOING THE DISTANCE. BELOW: HELMING THE *BRUNEI/SUNERGY* IN THE SOUTHERN OCEAN, 1997–98. RIGHT: VIEW FROM THE MAST OF *CHESSIE RACING* DURING THE SIXTH WHITBREAD STOPOVER, 1997–98.

THE BOC CHALLENGE AND THE VENDÉE GLOBE

Singlehanded racing is the aquatic version of marathon running, where the skipper has to draw from resources deep within himself for the endurance and stamina necessary to sail 30 days or more alone at sea.

Unlike the marathon runner, whose most important equipment is his shoes, a singlehanded sailor's equipment is a sailboat often as large as 60 feet (18m) and its accompanying systems—and it all has to be maintained continuously.

Joshua Slocum is considered the grandfather of singlehanded sailors. Between 1895 and 1898, Slocum singlehandedly circumnavigated the globe in a wooden boat, making stops along the way. Another 69 years elapsed before Francis Chichester completed a one-stop, singlehanded circumnavigation. Then, in 1969, Robin Knox-Johnston completed the first non-stop, singlehanded circumnavigation to win the Golden Globe Challenge.

Founded in 1982, the BOC Challenge is one of two singlehanded circumnavigation races. Its rival—and considered more difficult by some—is the Vendée Globe race. Instituted in 1989, the Vendée Globe is distinguished by its simpleness and extremeness; it is an all-out sprint departing and finishing in France whose basic requirements are leaving Antarctica to starboard and returning unassisted.

With no stops or assistance allowed in the global race, sailors must learn to fix anything that breaks on their boat, or learn to live without it. Their will must be strong enough to stitch themselves together after suffering a severe laceration in a knockdown, and then go on deck and stitch the sail together that ripped in the same accident.

The BOC has more stature worldwide because it led to a new generation of singlehanded sailors, as well as boats.

Many speed-enhancing features now key to today's singlehanded sailor were developed and refined in the heat of BOC competition—water ballast systems, autopilots, twin rudders, and the use of carbon fiber as a construction material in the hull and masts.

Skipper preparation for either race is as important as boat preparation. Getting as much pre-race rest is crucial, since solo sailing skippers get very little sleep.

A common routine sees many skippers catnapping for 30 to 40 minutes when they become tired. But in a span of 24 hours, they are lucky if they get six such naps. Constant vigilance is the name of this game.

In terms of pushing the limits of individual performance, both mentally and physically, singlehanded around the world yacht racing is one of the most challenging sports in terms of danger and time spent at risk.

Of course those that take part in the races will tell you it is for the love of being on the water that they do it.

GLOBAL SUPERSTAR. FAR LEFT: ELLEN MACARTHUR ON HER BOAT *KINGFISHER*, 90 MILES FROM THE FINISH LINE OF THE VENDÉE GLOBE CHALLENGE; ARRIVAL IN FRANCE; POPPING THE CORK.

SCUBA DIVING

THE MYSTERIES OF THE SEA HAVE LURED AVID DIVERS TO EXPERIENCE FIRST-HAND WHAT IT FEELS LIKE TO LIVE DEEP BENEATH THE WATER'S SURFACE. BUT MANY DIVERS HAVE PAID A HIGH COST FOR THE PRIVILEGE.

Those who pioneered modern scuba did so at great risk—our bodies were not meant to breathe under water, nor were they meant to breathe under the pressure of millions of pounds of liquid. As you go deeper into the sea, your body is no longer able to use the air you breathe as effectively as above the surface. As a result, hundreds of diving fatalities occur each year.

Man's search for a means to breathe underwater can be traced back to the ancient Romans, when early divers used a flotation device to support airhoses attached to leather helmets to provide oxygen. It was not until 1819 that deep-sea diving became a practical reality, when German inventor Augustus Siebein developed the bulky brass dive helmet linked to an air compressor back on the ship.

Nearly 130 years later, famous marine biologist Jacques Cousteau invented the aqualung together with fellow pioneer Emil Gagnan. The aqualung finally released divers from the restraints of air hoses and compressors, allowing them to swim freely through the water. The aqualung is unquestionably the most important invention in modern diving.

Since the aqualung's introduction, scuba (Self Contained Underwater Breathing Apparatus) has grown into a popular sport enjoyed by pleasure seekers, treasure hunters, researchers, and sportsmen globally. However, despite its popularity, scuba diving remains a dangerous sport that requires an in-depth knowledge of the effects extreme pressure can have on the body: how a diver absorbs air under these changing conditions, and a broad understanding of how to deal appropriately with the effects of pressure-breathing if accidents are to be avoided. One study of diving fatalities has revealed that the greatest danger lies not with the equipment but with the diver—almost all fatalities are due to human error.

There are other hazards. Hypothermia is a condition caused by the lowering of the body's core temperature, which can be fatal if prolonged. Sharp coral and rocks can cause injury, and strong underwater currents can separate dive partners—it's always advisable to dive in pairs at least—or, worse, sweep divers away from their support boat. Perhaps the most universally feared hazard is an encounter with a large shark or group of sharks. Smaller sharks can be docile if left alone, but they are never to be trusted. Larger

DOWN IN DAVY JONES' LOCKER.
BELOW: SCUBA DIVERS EXPLORE A CAVE OPENING;
RIGHT: THE DEVIL'S EYE OFF THE COAST OF FLORIDA IS AN UNDERWATER CAVE SYSTEM FULL OF SURPRISES.

sharks, such as tiger or great white sharks, are perpetually seeking food, and anything that swims is usually regarded as fair game.

Maladies associated with diving stem from how the body processes the air stored under pressure in the diver's tanks. As a diver swims deeper the body has to cope with increasing levels of pressure, measured in atmospheres. One "atmosphere" is the equivalent of the pressure exerted on the body at sea level, two atmospheres is double the pressure, and so on. As atmospheres increase, the pressure forces greater levels of breathed air into the bloodstream as gases.

Under controlled conditions at relatively shallow depths, this is not a problem until the diver surfaces. As the diver ascends, these gases—most notably nitrogen—start escaping from the bloodstream. The ascent must be controlled and slow enough to allow the gases to be released through normal exhalation through the diver's lungs. If the diver ascends too quickly, the gases can bubble out into the body tissue, causing muscular pain and bodily damage. It's a bit like the effect you see when you open a can or bottle of pressurized carbonated soda.

The results can be deadly, causing the body to curl up and convulse spastically—hence the name of "bends" for the condition. Non-fatal repercussions of the bends include coma, neurological disorders, and intense abdominal pain. Nitrogen—the main component of divers' compressed air—can have other side effect. One of the most alarming is "nitrogen narcosis." It is more common on deeper dives, where the increased pressure forces more nitrogen into the bloodstream, and takes the form of drowsiness—potentially lethal under water.

A decompression chamber—a large tank that can compress the air inside to several atmospheres—is commonly found on vessels used as dive-support stations.

Divers experiencing the bends are placed inside the decompression chamber and then quickly "returned" to the appropriate atmospheric pressure they were under in the water before the too-rapid ascent began. This allows the diver to complete the necessary decompression time and can halt the effects of the bends.

Diving using normal air mixtures—equivalent of the air we breathe every day—limits the depth and duration of dives. The deeper the dive, the less amount of time can be spent at the maximum depth. Knowing what the maximum lengths of time are for each depth is critical for diver safety.

Divers wanting to go deeper and stay down longer have to use different mixtures of air. Because of the extra requirements and the greater complexity of the process, deep dives are referred to as "technical" dives. Technical divers generally use enriched air such as "nitrox," a mixture with dramatically elevated amounts of oxygen. The use of enriched air mixtures is not recommended to any but the most experienced and well-trained of divers—Russian roulette is probably safer than technical diving without the required training and experience. A further system, called "rebreathing," utilizes a high-tech method of removing oxygen from exhaled air and recycling it for reuse.

Deep technical diving is the extreme end of scuba. Deep divers must have a rock solid understanding of the physiology and psychology of diving as well as strong stress management skills. Planning each dive is imperative so that decompression occurs at the proper rate and accidents are avoided.

The current record for deep diving using a non-enriched mixture was unofficially established in 1994 by Dr. Dan Manion, who dived to 942.5 feet (290m) and lost consciousness during his ascent. John Bennett, a technical diver from England, became the first man to go down 1,000 feet when he recorded a 1,001-feet (308m) dive off Puerto Galera, Philippines, in 2001. He died in March 2004 on a 146-feet (45m) dive off the coast of Korea.

Scuba is a dangerous sport, even for those seeking to dive for pleasure. Only those with enough training should dive. Even simple holiday excursions can result in tragedy. Extreme diving and depth record-setting is absolutely not recommended to anyone but the most expert divers, and even they are placing themselves at tremendous risk. Records are there to be broken and the depth record will surely be broken again at some point, but almost as certain is that lives will be lost in the process.

WONDERS OF THE DEEP. BELOW: LUNCH FROM A SHARK'S POV; CLOCKWISE (FROM TOP RIGHT): BOTTLENOSE DOLPHINS COSY UP TO A DIVER; JAGGED CORAL; WRECK-DIVING HOLDS GREAT APPEAL.

160

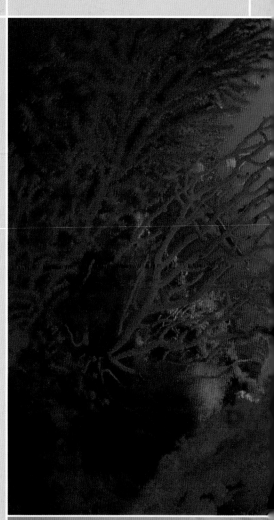

SNORKELING

FOR MOST PEOPLE SNORKELING IS JUST A HOLIDAY ACTIVITY. HOWEVER THERE IS A DARKER, DEEPER, MORE EXTREME TYPE OF SNORKELING THAT FEW WOULD TAKE UP WITHOUT A TANK, IF AT ALL.

Blue water hunters are a combination of freediver and spearfisher, and swim down slowly into the water, careful not to disturb any of the larger, and tastier, inhabitants.

The diver must maintain a state of calm, equilibrium and heightened awareness in order to get a glimpse of the big fish they seek to catch. Quiet, methodical movements are the only way extreme snorkelers will avoid scaring their prey.

Better divers release the seal around their snorkels and fill their mouths with water to prevent any air bubbles from alerting fish to their presence. They must constantly swivel around 180 degrees to stay prepared for approaching fish, and the occasional shark.

Incredible focus is required to notice oncoming fish and potentially unfriendly sealife in the distance before being seen, giving enough time to prepare for the shot. Divers keep a lookout for schools of bait fish that draw larger predators, and hope for "the big one" to show up.

Divers can effectively lure fish closer by staying horizontal and looking head on as they approach. If the fish feel the diver is as small as his profile, they may become curious and seek a closer look.

Other methods of luring fish include making croaking noises and setting bait or artificial lures.

Divers typically rise to the surface for around 45 seconds before submerging again, and try to stay down as long as possible, usually 60 seconds or more. They try to position themselves for optimum shooting when a fish is in the area. The best angle for a shot is downward and around 10–15 feet (3–4.5m) away. Quiet divers blend into their environment and get close enough to be in range.

Divers carry an assortment of gear on each trip out, including a wetsuit, snorkel and mask, fins, and a hand spear or spear gun. Additional equipment includes a weightbelt, dive knife, gear bag, and back-up items. A typical spear gun measures around 5–6 feet (1.5–1.8m) in length using 6-foot spears made from stainless steel. The butt end of the gun is weighted to afford the diver better balance and more control over the gun, as well as additional ballast to help them stay submerged. The ballast consists of lead shot which can be added or removed if needed.

Extreme snorkelers do not generally seek out small prey, but are in search of larger stuff, in the 200–500 lb (90–225 kg) category. Blue- and yellow-fin tuna, black marlin, and other larger game fish separate this style of spear fishing from the tamer stuff. Many divers can tell stories of landing huge fish, only to be nearly drowned in the tow that ensued. It is therefore highly critical that the diver hit the target in the right spot and score a quick kill. Aside from the risk of a long battle while being towed, there is the very real risk of a physical confrontation with their catch, which can be a life or death struggle. Consider a 500 lb marlin coming full speed with its spear shaped nose pointed straight at you.

The sport is certainly not for the tame. It does, however, provide a new perspective on a sport that is relatively safe and rarely considered extreme.

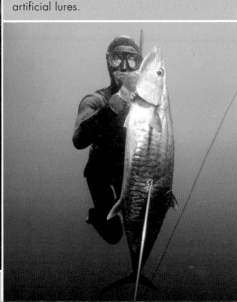

SOFTLY SOFTLY CATCHY MONKEY—STEALTH IS THE VITAL INGREDIENT FOR A GOOD SNORKELING HAUL. FAR LEFT: A SNORKELER STEADIES HIMSELF BEFORE FIRING; LEFT: HANGING ON TO A SPANISH MACKEREL.

SPEED SAILING

ONCE SPEED MEANT SAILORS COULD TRAVEL FARTHER FOR BIGGER AND BETTER CATCHES. TODAY, THE QUEST FOR SPEED IS ABOUT ESTABLISHING NEW LEVELS OF PERFORMANCE AND REWRITING THE RECORD BOOKS.

Speed sailing for sport has brought with it most of the current high-technology equipment and space-age materials now common in everyday sailing. Sailing faster requires lighter watercraft that hardly resemble the sailboats of even a decade ago—the vessel currently holding the speed sailing record cannot be turned, and can only sail in one direction! Speed sailing is a highly specialized sport requiring highly specialized designs. The only goal is to accelerate within a straight, closed course, and pass through a section of that course at maximum velocity in hope of recording a new speed record. To break the record in practice is only momentarily satisfying, as no speed is official without being recorded at a sanctioned event site, with official timekeepers present. So the object is to design a boat that can break records on any given day in any reasonable breeze—official events and perfect conditions do not always coincide.

For years the record books were filled with catamarans, and every successful attempt merely edged out the previous record. Catamarans are sailboats with two slender hulls that slice through the water, offering little resistance other than the inescapable surface tension between their hulls and the water. Going faster meant minimizing the amount of hull surface that contacted the water and maximizing the amount of horsepower the sails could generate. This meant huge rigs carrying tremendous sails on hulls that barely sustained the loads placed on them. This led to terribly overpowered sailboats that self-destructed under the forces they generated more often than they set records.

In the Eighties, the records established by catamarans were suddenly destroyed by tiny, specially designed sailboards which were hardly in contact with the water at speed and required sails small enough that they could be supported by the sailor. Sailboards owned the world speed record for nearly a decade.

Then in 1992 a new and radical sailing hydrofoil shattered the record by traveling at 50.02 knots on an official course at the French Trench outside of Calais, France. The Trifoiler designed by Californian Greg Ketterman was much smaller and lighter than previous record setters, with the obvious exception of sailboards. The Trench is famous for its strong sideways winds and narrow, protected waters that ensure a nearly perfect flat water surface. The Trifoiler reduced speed-limiting surface to only a small fraction of what had been previously reached during years of effort.

CATCH THE WIND. BELOW AND RIGHT: THE YELLOW PAGES-SPONSORED *ENDEAVOUR* WAS DESIGNED SPECIALLY TO BREAK SPEED RECORDS. THE CREW SAT IN A TINY COMPARTMENT ON ONE OF THE WINGS.

This record-setting design did have a limiting factor, and that was the efficiency of the wing-like foils that lift the boat out of the water at speed. These create speed-limiting drag at the top end of their performance, making it impossible for them to travel faster. An Australian design dubbed "Yellow Pages," named after the craft's sponsor, used a design similar in appearance to Ketterman's Trifoiler, however rather than using hydrofoils Yellow Pages used small skis to ride on. This both greatly reduced the surface tension that earlier catamaran designs suffered and eliminated the top-end performance limits of the Trifoiler's.

Yellow Pages was a speed-record-specific design incapable of turning or sailing in more than one direction.

But it was fast enough to edge out the Trifoiler for top spot in the record books. Because it used skis to ride on, it was a step back in the direction of the speed record-setting sailboards. But, because it used a large sail held up by stays (wires), it could carry far more sail area than any sailboard, and therefore had a tremendous horsepower advantage.

The quest for the world speed sailing record continues. Somewhere, now, there is a designer working hard to redefine the limits of wind-driven speed on water. Given that land-sailing vehicles are capable of exceeding 100 mph (160kph), it is surely only a matter of time before sailboats will reach such speeds. When that occurs the way we travel over water will be forever changed. This is bound to expand the distances sailing vessels can cover, since unlike land sailcraft which are limited by the terrain available to cover, speed sailcraft will have an endless supply of water, and the distances traveled will be limited only by their design's ability to deal with a variety of surface conditions.

BUILT FOR SPEED. BELOW AND RIGHT: THE AUSTRALIAN BOAT *MACQUARIE INNOVATION* WAS DESIGNED TO BREAK THE MAGIC 50 KNOT BARRIER. PICTURED HERE IN TESTS AT SANDY POINT, TASMANIA.

SURFING

MANY PEOPLE DAYDREAM OF RIDING EFFORTLESSLY DOWN THE FACE OF A BIG WAVE, YET MOST DON'T UNDERSTAND THAT SURFING IS LESS ABOUT THE RIDE THAN IT IS ABOUT LIFE ITSELF...

Ask any surfer to explain what it feels like to surf and they will tell you to try it for yourself, since as one surfer eloquently stated, "trying to explain surfing to a non-surfer is like trying to explain sex to a virgin." There is something mystical to the entire process of surfing, something that can only be experienced.

Each wave at every surf spot is as different from the last one as one snowflake is from another. Consider that each wave has traveled hundreds of miles to get to the shore, and has met countless forces that ultimately determine how it will break and when.

Every swell is created by open ocean storms that blow the water into lines. While the lines are rolling through open ocean they are known as swell, it is only when they arrive at the shore that they become waves. Each swell contains thousands, even millions, of waves that vary in speed, angle of approach and size. In that sense, surfing is much like life, with a different twist and turn around each corner, whether it is a personality or a circumstance one is dealing with, each is unique and requires a unique response. As in surfing, the proper response means harmony, and the wrong response can be devastating.

Surfing began centuries ago in the Pacific Island cultures where its roots can be traced to the beginnings of Polynesian society. By the seventeenth century, surfing was a widely accepted aspect of both the ruling and working classes in Hawaii. Surfing was to these people a part of their secular lives, replete with surfing gods, sacred rituals, and a strong set of social values all linked to surfing.

Early Hawaiians took their surfing very seriously. Hawaiian chiefs could declare any of their favourite surfing spots "Kapu," meaning they were off limits to all but the chief and his friends. Chiefs would direct their subjects to bring only the finest wood from the cold highland regions of the island. The best craftsmen would be entrusted with shaping the chief's board from the wood, often from the prized koa or the wiliwili tree. Commoners would ride boards of much less exotic wood. Yet regardless of the value of the surfboard, it was always treated with respect. A proper surf building ritual was always performed out of respect for the surf gods, so as to provide the owner with good waves and the safety of being protected from harm.

Lieutenant James King of the British Royal Navy first described surfing to "the civilized world" in 1779. He remarked that he'd seen Hawaiians surfing massive "boomers" at Kealakekua Bay. Typical of the awestruck explorers of the period, he described surfing as "most perilous and extraordinary, altogether astonishing and scarcely to be credited."

Surfing, of course, continued and eventually, over 150 years later, with the legendary Duke Kahanamoku as its ambassador, grew to become the international force in water sports it is today. Duke was the inventor of the front crawl swimming stroke and the first recognized star of the surfing community. He was so famous that Hollywood stars flocked to Hawaii to meet and be photographed with him.

Duke is credited with being the founding father of modern surfing, and organised the first surf club in the world, the Hui Nalu. "Da Hui" still thrives today and is known throughout the world. Its membership consists of the biggest names in the surfing world, past and present, and loyalty among its members is extremely strong. Other notable surf clubs formed by influential Hawaiians include the Outrigger Club, and the Healani.

Surfing reached California in the Fifties where it spawned a cultural revolution, inspiring the popularity of the beach lifestyle that was reflected in the surf music of Dick Dale and the Beach Boys. Surf films glorifying the Hawaiian and Californian surf culture became wildly popular at the same time. Amazingly, though, it was Thomas Edison who filmed surfers at Honolulu's famed Waikiki Beach in 1898, who produced some of the very first surf movies.

SURFING IS THE ORIGINAL EXTREME SPORT. LEFT: RIDING A BOARD THROUGH THE WAVES GOES BACK TO THE BEGINNINGS OF POLYNESIAN SOCIETY.

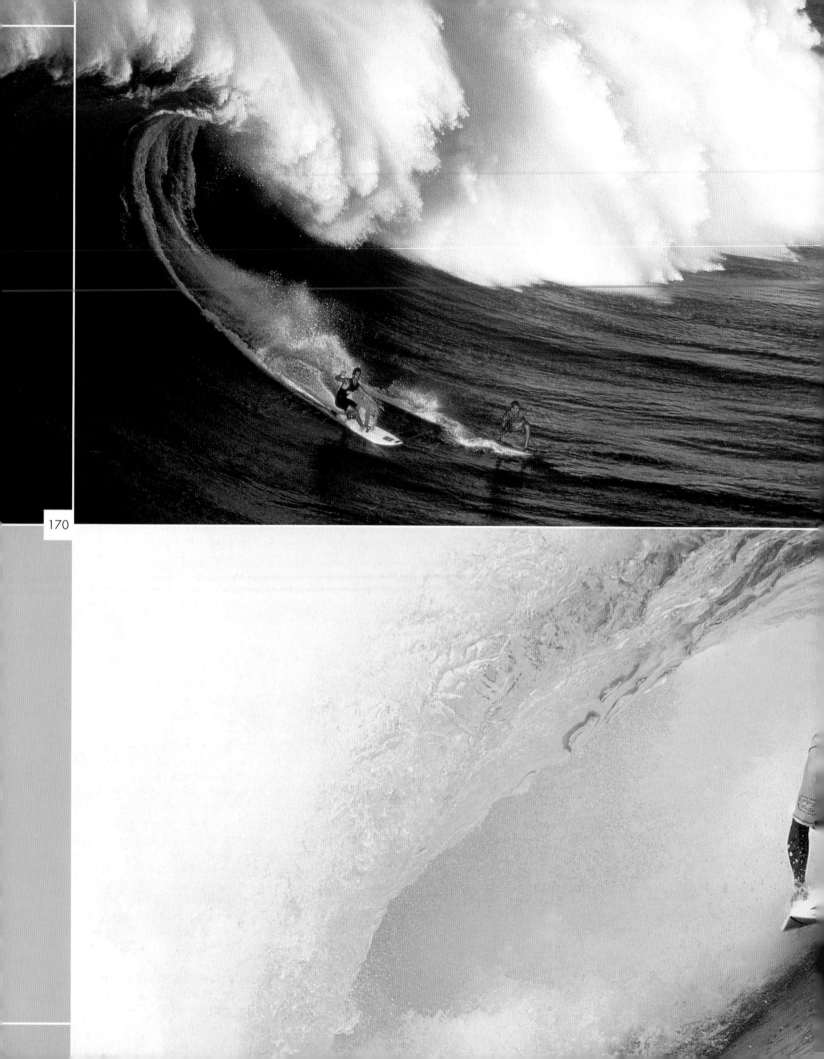

Surf movies gained a wider audience with the work of pioneers like Bruce Brown, who captured the authentic surfing scene with his first feature film, *The Big Surf*, in 1943. His most notable film was *The Endless Summer*, which followed a few nomadic surfers on a quest for the perfect wave. Its sequel, *The Endless Summer II*, released in 1994, has inspired an international following similar to that of his first film. Like all extreme sports, it has been the mediums of video (and, more recently, DVD) that has accelerated the progression of surfing, as people round the world are able to study and emulate their heroes. Surfing looks brilliant on film and tape, and it wouldn't be wrong to say that surfing pioneered the extreme sports video.

Modern surfing has progressed tremendously since the days of massive wooden boards ridden by the pioneers of surfing in Hawaii and the Polynesian islands. Today's surfboards vary enormously in size and shape. Professional surfers own a "quiver" (collection) of different boards designed to perform in all ranges of surf conditions. Shorter boards in lengths of 5–7 feet (1.5–2m) are used primarily in smaller waves for maneuverability and work well with the shape of the faces on smaller waves.

Short boards have been credited for developing many of today's freestyle tricks. These moves are unlike any seen in the history of surfing, with many taking inspiration from what has been done in skateboarding. Surfers have mastered aerials to the extent that leaders in the field like Cory Lopez, Andy and Bruce Irons and Kelly Slater can consistently land 6-8 ft (2-2.5m) airs, 360 degree spins, grabs and even inverts. These ridiculously technical tricks have come to redefine the boundaries of modern surfing.

"Gun" surfboards of between 7–11 feet (2.4-3.4m) are used for bigger and more powerful waves. Their longer profiles give added edge, holding in big surf where speeds are considerably greater than in lesser conditions, their higher volume also enables surfers to paddle into the waves.

Big-wave surfing is experiencing a renaissance, with new and hazardous spots like Teahupoo in Tahiti and Cortez Bank, an offshore reef off the pacific coast of California, competing for attention with some of the more recognizable big-wave locations like Waimea on the North Shore of Oahu, Mavericks in Northern California and the Islands of Todos Santos off Baja. Mavericks gained international recognition for its extreme conditions when self-styled, big-wave surf star

CLOCKWISE (FROM TOP LEFT): LAIRD HAMILTON (RIGHT) AND PETE CABRINA, HAWAII; HAMILTON AGAIN; KELLY SLATER IN THE BILLABONG SURF CONTEST.

Mark Foo lost his life after being engulfed by one of Mavericks's moderate-sized waves. What makes Mavericks so dangerous are the jagged rocks that line the bay, the thick seaweed in the impact zone and the water temperature. Coping with big waves is hard enough without a thick rubber wetsuit, boots, a hood and gloves on!

Different waves have different hazards and at present the title "Heaviest wave on earth" belongs to the Teahupoo reef in Tahiti. As the wave approaches the reef from deep water, it begins to suck the water off the reef until a giant standing wall of water looms over it. Because the water has flooded off the reef with the pull of the wave it creates a pit that is below sea level. As the wave begins to break, it looks and sounds as if the entire ocean is throwing itself onto the coral. It is here that Laird Hamilton rode the Millennium wave: arguably the most dangerous wave ever surfed.

"Longboards" are now making a comeback in surfing after years in the shadow of the supposed revolutionary short surfboards. For many years, long boards had been considered to be for "old men" and "kooks" (surfer lingo for novices with no skills and even less water knowledge). Now surfers are getting new, almost nostalgic, respect for long boards as surfers recognize that they offer a different skill set that can help surfers to become more rounded in their ability. They are also, lest we forget, the most valuable teaching device in the surfing world and everyone has to start somewhere.

The newest entrants to the realm of surfboard design are the "tow-in" boards used to surf the biggest and heaviest waves in the world. The sport was pioneered by Hawaiian surfing legend Laird Hamilton and a crew of watermen who pride themselves on their all-round ability in all aspects of water culture. Hamilton and other notables, including Dave Kalama, Peter Cabrina and Brock Little, had all mastered windsurfing when it arrived in the islands and, as its popularity faded, the crew returned their focus to surfing. But they brought with them one valuable asset: foot straps.

The group began experimenting with short and narrow board designs that could be towed behind a Jet Ski. They found that without the need to paddle into waves, the size and volume of the boards could be massively reduced. Interestingly, they did need the boards to retain their weight, so that they would stick to the surface and not bounce on the massive chops they encountered while riding down the faces of huge waves.

They found that, by being towed, they

173

CLOCKWISE (FROM TOP LEFT): THE WONDERFUL WAVES OF HAWAII; PETE CABRINA, ONE OF THE TOP TOW-IN SURFERS; HOLLY BECK AT THE U.S. OPEN, 2003.

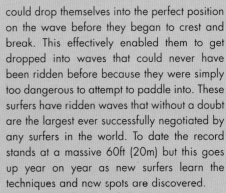

could drop themselves into the perfect position on the wave before they began to crest and break. This effectively enabled them to get dropped into waves that could never have been ridden before because they were simply too dangerous to attempt to paddle into. These surfers have ridden waves that without a doubt are the largest ever successfully negotiated by any surfers in the world. To date the record stands at a massive 60ft (20m) but this goes up year on year as new surfers learn the techniques and new spots are discovered.

The most famous of the tow-in spots is a particularly dangerous reef, aptly named "Jaws." The mushroom-shaped reef, located on Maui in the Hawaiian Islands, creates a wave that comes in like a freight train out of deep water and breaks in a crescent shape. The reef at Jaws is the first thing the swell hits after building up power over thousands of miles of open ocean.

There is no question that a mistake here can end in a fatality. The waves are so powerful that it is not uncommon for them to hold a surfer down for 60 seconds or more in a wipeout. Surfers are reportedly experimenting with miniature breathing tanks to provide much needed air in the event of a deadly hold-down. But for the moment, the elite crew of surfers who choose to surf here train by running around on the seabed with giant boulders to improve their underwater fitness.

Big-wave and tow-in surfing could certainly be regarded as the future of surfing, but with so many different areas of the sport progressing at such a rate, it is impossible to predict where it will head next. There are already wave parks around the world that create a fake standing wave of up to eight feet high. Is it impossible to believe we will be seeing Kelly Slater and Laird Hamilton's kids doing double backflips on an 80-foot standing wave in the middle of Arizona in 2025?

CLOCKWISE (FROM LEFT): KELLY SLATER IN ACTION; DAVID JENKINS CATCHES A PERFECT BARREL WAVE; THE CALM AT THE CENTRE OF THE POUNDING WAVES.

WAKEBOARDING

WAKEBOARDING IS A RELATIVELY NEW SPORT BUT IT CAN BE LINKED TO WATERSKIING, SURFING, SKATEBOARDING, AND SNOWBOARDING, AND IT IS REDEFINING BOAT-TOWED SPORTS.

The concept of towing a surfboard behind either a boat in the water or a car on the beach on waveless days is as old as modern surfing. The need to ride on a board drives many "sideways" sports enthusiasts to try whatever they need to get out and ride on their boards. That's how skateboarding began, and later windsurfing and snowboarding. For decades, if there was no surf, surfers were known to grab a line and get pulled by a boat or even by a truck running onshore.

In 1985, San Diego surfer Tony Finn created and developed a waterski/surfboard he called the Skurfer. It was narrower than a surfboard and riders could do snowboard-like turns behind their boats. Soon, with the addition of footstraps, skurfers were riding their boards and performing many of the same maneuvers snowboarders were doing. That same year, Texas surfer Jimmy Redmond added footstraps to another early wakeboard design.

The early skurfers pushed hard and began getting big air and pulling off dynamic moves, however the appeal didn't grow far outside of the community of strong skiers because the Skurfer's narrow and highly buoyant design made it difficult to master. In 1990 waterski pioneer Hugh O'Brien gathered together many top surfers to create a board design that had many of the performance characteristics of a good surfboard.

The "Hyperlite" design that was created had neutral buoyancy, and was compression-molded like the waterskis O'Brien's H.O. Sports company was mass-producing. The neutral buoyancy design and thin profile rails (board edges) allowed the Hyperlite design to carve shorter, slalom-like turns than the Skurfer. The design also made getting up and mastering the board easier, growing the appeal of what would be called the wakeboard.

Indents called "phasers" were added to help break up the water flow under the board, making the board feel "looser" (less stuck to the water) and making high-air landings softer on the rider. Phasers were borrowed from windsurfer and surfboard shapers seeking to create the same loose feel for their designs.

Wakeboarding soon exploded in popularity and continues to do so today. The sport is reported to have grown by as much as 400 per cent in recent years, adding a professional tour and a governing body to help it along the way. One of the reasons is that wakeboarding's top professionals are pushing their sport to new limits on a daily basis. The best have added new elements to wakeboarding that come straight out of skateboarding street style and snowboarding freestyle. These riders are doing grinds off obstacles like channel buoys and docks, and are even jumping on and over rock outcroppings where available.

Wakeboard binding systems have developed rapidly to deal with the added forces riders are putting on their equipment. Initially, the bindings used were simply upgraded or modified waterski-style. The new bindings offer tremendously more support and grip to hold riders on their boards. In fact, the new designs are so snug that liquid soap is standard in getting into or out of the bindings. The reasoning is obvious: create new moves that your equipment can't deal with and you wipe out.

Wakeboarding parks are now being created where once waterskiing parks existed. Wakeboarders are discovering new uses for the overhead pull systems that resemble ski lifts, and now use the added lift to soar up and around the courses, doing spins and other moves never before seen at ski parks.

Newer and younger riders are getting into the sport, and it is certain that they will bring with them even more innovative approaches to wakeboarding.

Wakeboarding is poised to do the same thing for waterskiing and tow-behind water sports that snowboarding did to revitalize the ski industry. It also provides a real indication of where board sports are headed... sideways.

FAR FROM A DRAG. NEAR RIGHT: WAYNE MOWER HANGS OUT BEHIND HIS SKIBOAT; FAR RIGHT: MARK KENNY WAKEBOARDING IN NSW, AUSTRALIA.

WHITEWATER

TO PROVE YOUR METTLE AGAINST THE MOST VIOLENT OF NATURE'S FORCES— THE FURY OF MOVING WATER—IS TO PARTICIPATE IN ONE OF THE MOST ADRENALINE-PUMPING OF EXTREME SPORTS.

There are varying degrees of difficulty to consider when choosing which watercraft best suits the needs of the rider. The first and least difficult method of getting down whitewater is via a raft, which can be easily found for hire near any thriving river community. Whitewater rafting is a big business, as it offers the opportunity to enjoy the rush of the ride without most of the risks associated.

Which is not to say whitewater rafting is easy and lacking danger. Reputable tour operators offer quality guidance and top rate equipment, including two of the most important pieces of gear needed, a helmet and a life vest. Any time the river is entered on a watercraft, there are risks, and every year, people are seriously injured or killed on rivers all over the world while on rafts. Having said that, if whitewater is appealing, try a rafting expedition first to see how you like it.

Next in difficulty would be the canoe, which due to the open nature of the design, offers little protection from a capsize. Many canoeists are qualified to run rivers of sizeable power, however, canoes do not offer the "righting" performance (returning the boat to a rightside-up position) necessary in big rapids. Canoes are less stable than rafts and require tremendous balance skills to ride through areas of whitewater.

The boogieboard, aka riverboard, a device first developed to ride beach surf while lying down, is a new entry into the whitewater-running category. Many whitewater enthus-iasts, seeking to push the limits and try a new thrill began riding the foam boards in whitewater with success. One of the pioneers, Bob Carlson, now sells his Carlson Riverboards all over the world, many to top river runners. While certainly easier to stay on top of and right after rolling over, the riverboard is far more extreme than rafting or canoeing. On a riverboard the rider is completely exposed to

WHITE KNUCKLE RIDE THE WAY NATURE INTENDED. RAFTING, THOUGH HARD WORK, IS THE BEST WAY OF ENJOYING THE RUSH WITH THE FEWEST RISKS.

the elements without the protection of a boat's hull to ward off jagged rocks and absorb some of the shock the rapids can hand out.

The most extreme method of getting down a river, however, is on a kayak. Kayaks offer a completely enclosed hull design that allows the paddler to sit in the opening of the hull and seal themselves in using a neoprene skirt. Because the paddler is able to capsize and right the boat without filling the hull with water, they can handle practically any degree of whitewater. The act of righting a capsized kayak is called an "Eskimo roll," since it was created by the Eskimos. Because of the severely cold water, Eskimos have to stay dry and be able to right themselves without doing what is now called a "wet exit," meaning escaping the capsized boat.

For many reasons, doing a wet exit is the last thing a paddler wants to do unless they absolutely must. First, outside the kayak the paddler is immediately exposed to a multitude of dangers, from massive "hydrolics" (sections of the river where tons of water are being pushed downward), to sharp rocks, submerged logs, and other unknowns. Second, once outside the hull, the paddler's only flot-ation is their body and their life vest. The drop in flotation makes the possibility of the paddler being driven downward onto a hidden obstacle far greater. More than a few paddlers die each year from simply getting their foot stuck under a rock, and then being dragged under by the current. These two examples should be enough to illustrate why being able to do an Eskimo roll at will is essential to paddling heavy water.

Kayaks are incredibly maneuverable because of their low buoyancy and highly "rockered" shapes, which vary from design to design. Rocker refers to the curve in the hull from front (bow) to back (stern). The more rocker in the hull, the more maneuverable the kayak. Different designs accommodate different performance characteristics. One example is a slalom kayak. Designed to race through a series of gates, the hull is highly rockered, with sharp,

angular projections along the top of the deck that serve to provide greater sideways stability, helping the paddler get across the current to the next gate more easily.

Another is a low-buoyancy "rodeo"-style, or trick kayak, which is a minimally buoyant design used in trick contests. The reduced-volume rodeo design allows the paddler to spin the kayak around on its ends effortlessly, as well as performing a number of other tricks. Low-buoyancy kayaks are also the preferred design for high waterfall drops that some of the more radical paddlers enjoy. Waterfall paddling is probably the most dangerous of all the whitewater activities, depending on the distance of the drop. Small waterfalls of 5–10 feet (1.5–3m) constitute normal conditions in extreme whitewater.

The larger waterfalls that the top extreme paddlers drop into can exceed 50 feet (15m). Clearly the opportunity for disaster exists at these heights, and the paddler must land the kayak end first, either bow or stern. Landing any other way results in "flatting out" (landing hard on the entire surface of the hull) which can severely injure a paddler. This is the kayaking equivalent of a belly flop. If the paddler lands on the end, the kayak dives down into the water with a relatively soft landing. Obviously these types of stunts are reserved for top experts only.

Regardless of the type of watercraft used, there is a system of classifying the level of difficulty for each section of a river. The level of difficulty varies from day to day as the amount of water traveling through a section can radically alter the whitewater character-istics. Rivers are measured in cubic feet, so a river traveling at 3,000 cfs (cubic feet per second) will behave quite differently on a day when it is traveling at 10,000 cfs. Snowmelt or torrential rains can dramatically change a river, and in the case of torrential rain it can happen instantly. Therefore, it is important that river riders are aware of not only the weather immediately around them, but also the weather conditions upstream.

Rivers are rated on a scale of 1–6. The higher the number, the greater the degree of difficulty. It is important to acknowledge that river sections can vary dramatically in difficulty, and it is not uncommon for a river to change from class 1 to class 6 within a matter of meters. Again, it is vital to get local information on the river before going downstream. The following outlines the classification system:

- CLASS I – easy, occasionally small rapids with few obstacles
- CLASS II – moderate, small rapids and waves which are easily navigated
- CLASS III – difficult, rapids, hazards, and irregular waves which should be scouted from shore ahead of time; complex maneuvers will be required
- CLASS IV – very difficult, long, large rapids and falls with hazards which must be scouted; precise moves will be required, including rolls; rescues will be difficult
- CLASS V – has extremely difficult, violent rapids and falls with narrow routes and many dangerous hazards; experts only!
- CLASS VI – nearly impossible, routes difficult to identify; only to be attempted by teams of top expert paddlers following all possible precautions

It's useful to know a few of the terms commonly used in whitewater. Beam is the widest part of the boat. Thwart is a support which runs across the width of the boat. Blade is the thin cross-section, wide profile part of the paddle that passes through the water and provides thrust. Shaft is the "handle" of the paddle gripped by the paddler. Draw is a paddle stroke 90 degrees to the direction of travel to pull the boat sideways. J-stroke is a paddle stroke that ends in a steering maneuver. River-left refers the side of the river as it looks to the paddler, while river-right speaks for itself.

WHOAY AND UP SHE RISES. LEFT: THERE'S NOTHING LIKE BEING IN A GROUP FOR SHARING THE THRILLS; BELOW: THERE AGAIN, YOU COULD GO SOLO...

No one is certain as to exactly when the first boat resembling a canoe or kayak was built. The Eskimos of north America and northeastern Asia are felt to have been the originators of the modern kayak. Early Eskimo kayaks were built of lightweight wooden frames wrapped in seal or caribou skin. These kayaks held one or two paddlers, and were used primarily for fishing.

Modern recreational canoeing and kayaking got their start after a Scottish barrister named John MacGregor designed a boat he called the "Rob Roy."

The boat was based on the Eskimo kayak, and he used the designs between 1845 and 1869 to explore many of the waterways of Europe. He wrote and lectured extensively regarding his explorations.

MacGregor founded the Royal Canoe Club in 1866, with the Prince of Wales as Commodore, a post he retained until he was crowned king. The New York Canoe Club was founded in 1871 in response to the success of the Royal Canoe Club.

Kayaking became an Olympic sport in 1936, and remains so today. Twelve of the 16 events are sprints held on flat water. Slalom kayaking is held in whitewater, and requires paddlers to traverse a series of gates, both upcurrent and downcurrent.

This event is widely regarded as one of the most physically demanding paddling sports because it requires strength, lightning fast maneuverability skills, and a keen ability to read the currents.

Whitewater as a sport, whether as featured in the Olympic Games or for fun, is one of the purest forms of play in a natural and changing environment.

It is a great way to get out into the wilderness and enjoy an adrenaline-charged workout, and is one extreme sport that almost everyone can enjoy at some level.

LEFT: WHITEWATER RACES ARE BECOMING MORE AND MORE POPULAR; BELOW: TEAMWORK CAN GIVE YOU A TREMENDOUS FEELING OF SATISFACTION.

WINDSURFING

SINCE IT WAS FIRST INTRODUCED TO READERS IN A 1965 EDITION OF *POPULAR SCIENCE* MAGAZINE, WINDSURFING HAS DEVELOPED INTO ONE OF THE MOST ICONIC EXTREME SPORTS.

Californian surfer and businessman Hoyle Schweitzer and aeronautical engineer Jim Drake invented the sailboard. Schweitzer reportedly conceived of the idea of putting a sail on a surfboard while Drake created the articulating sail rig that made the concept feasible. The two promptly applied for, and were granted, patents on their design and began the company that would be known worldwide as Windsurfer.

The original windsurfer was a 12-foot (3.65m) long, heavy board made from pressure-molded ABS plastic. The boards were rough and their sail rigs were unrefined, using wooden booms (what the sailor holds onto) and inefficient sails. However, the sensation for early sailors was incredibly exciting and unlike anything any other sailing vessel could offer, including fast and exciting catamarans. Soon there were Windsurfers everywhere and races were organized by enthusiasts.

New equipment was developed, including "harnesses" that allowed windsurfers to "hook in and hold on" for longer sessions with less arm fatigue.

The early harnesses had hooks on the chest that grabbed lines tied to the booms of the sail rig. Back fatigue and injuries resulted in a new "seat" harness designed to give better leverage and control over the rig, and decrease stresses placed on the sailor's back. But a problem the harness created was that a sailor hit by a large gust of wind, or off balance, could be catapulted forward and slammed into the water, or worse, into the board itself.

Harnesses now come as standard equipment for any windsurfer, however the opportunity to get slammed is still one of the hazards of the sport.

Hawaiian surfers made the first groundbreaking modifications to Windsurfers. When they started adding foot straps to their boards, modern wave sailing was born.

Early pioneers like Robby Naish, who was 15 when he won his first world title, are still leading figures of windsurfing today, and have also helped pioneer offshoot sports such as kiteboarding.

Foot straps delivered a new dimension of control to windsurfing, allowing sailors to stay on their boards in winds that would have previously thrown them and as a result, getting "slammed" became far less frequent.

Being able to gain a more secure footing also let sailors break into new speed territory. Soon enough the advances in equipment and ease of control in high-wind sailing made light to moderate winds look boring and the bigger heavy boards became the dinosaurs of windsurfing.

As with many speed-oriented sports, lighter means faster, and stiffer means better control. Sailboarders seeking to sail in extreme conditions of high wind, or high wind and surf, found that, once their boards were planing (riding on top of the water rather than through it), they no longer required the giant surface area of the big boards.

In fact, big hulls became unstable in high winds since the wind would continuously seek to rip the board away from the water and sailor. Smaller boards were made lighter, and those that could get started on them could run circles around other sailors.

The catch, however, was that, the smaller the boards became, the less buoyancy they offered, to the point at which they no longer supported the sailor's weight unless they were moving and could ride on top of water.

Riders wishing to sail these "sinkers" had to learn to do a "water start." In a water start, because the board cannot float with the sailor on it, the sailor lies in the water waiting for the sail to pick them up onto the board.

As the sailor gets lifted up, the board begins moving, increasing its ability to support his weight. As the board accelerates, it planes (rides on top) on the water's surface, and is able to travel with little resistance. The sailor

THE ANSWER IS BLOWING IN THE WIND. RIGHT: THERE ARE ALMOST NO LIMITS TO THE MANEUVERS YOU CAN PERFORM ON A WINDSURFER.

must keep the sail properly trimmed (adjusted) to maximize the amount of force the available wind can give to move the board. Therefore, the better the sailor is at trimming the sail, the faster the board will travel.

Top experts can get their boards to travel at their maximum velocity for the wind and water conditions. The rest is a matter of skill and handling ability. An expert can steer the board with light foot movements and weight transfer, using the board's rails (edges) to carve turns in the same manner as surfing.

Board designs vary as to their maneuverability and top speed potential. Boards with straighter shapes and sharp (close to 90 degree angle) rails release the water from the bottom of the board better and attain higher speeds, but are more difficult to turn, as they have a tendency to skip out of a hard turn. Boards with rounder shapers and loose (rounded) rails are highly maneuverable but don't go as fast.

Boards also vary in rocker (the amount the bottom curves from the tip to tail of the board). Rocker placement varies from board to board. Boards with more rocker in the tail will be slower but more maneuverable, while boards with less tail rocker will plane quicker and go faster.

Each board designer places rocker in different places determined by the performance desired, and each windsurfer prefers a different feel and shape. Early "short" board designs looked more like surfboards than today's top shapes.

Board buoyancy is measured by volume, so less volume means less flotation. Designers shift the volume around in their boards, placing more or less in the tip or tail dramatically affects the performance.

Volume placement has been the biggest area of development in windsurfing design over the last ten years. Short boards started

RIDERS ON THE STORM. RIGHT: JEAN-LUC VASSE OF FRANCE TAKES ON THE BIG WAVES OF HOOKIPA, HAWAII; BELOW: ROBBY NAISH, COOL UNDER PRESSURE.

out with massive amounts of volume in the tail. One early design by top windsurfer Ken Winner actually had a hump through the middle of the rear deck of the board, and a pointy front. Designers gradually reduced the volume in the back of the boards, moving it forward under the mast base.

The volume-forward shapes were the predominant style of short boards until the early Nineties, when designers discovered they could reduce the length and increase board performance by centering the volume under the sailor, much like Winner's early design, but without the hump.

The "no nose" designs have greatly reduced size at the front, with much of the rail shape occurring farther back in the board. Essentially what they've done is to take a very short board and put volume and width under the sailor to create a moderately short board. Either way, these boards are a vast improvement over designs only a few years old.

Getting airborne when you are attached to a giant wing isn't that hard, what is however, is controlling it on the way down. Experts have developed jumps that not only use the sail to get airborne but also to initiate and even stall rotations and flips in midair. What windsurfers can do in the air has changed dramatically over the years as equipment has changed and sailors have redefined the limits of performance.

Tricks like "forward loops" (front flips) are now standard fare for top accomplished sailors. In a forward loop, the sailor goes as fast as possible into a wave and, while airborne, pulls hard on the boom with the back hand; this has the effect of throwing the sail power into the front of the rig and pulling the sailor, board and rig into a front flip. This highly technical trick is amazing to watch, not least because the sailor is effectively recreating the same sensation as being slammed, but in the air!

One of the best technical advances in windsurfing was the introduction of the R.A.F. (Rotating Aerodynamic Foil) and Camber-Inducing batten systems. The R.A.F. system was the first to be introduced, and it allowed sails to take on more rigid, wing-like shapes when rigged by adding stiff horizontal battens made of fibreglass across the sail. This design made sails far easier to handle in high and gusty wind conditions because they created smoother shapes and a more manageable rig with less drag.

Drag pulls on a sail, sometimes violently, and decreases topend velocity. Camber Inducers were then introduced when sail-

CLOCKWISE (FROM TOP RIGHT): RALF BACHSCHUSTER AND PATRICE BELBEOCH; PARTING OF THE WAYS; IN FORMATION; FRANCE'S JENNE DE ROSNAY.

188

makers added enough length to the sail's battens to connect them to the mast that supports the sail. Camber Inducers allowed sailmakers to design rigid shapes that are incredibly wind-efficient almost like solid wings. It was the innovation of the Camber Inducer that eventually helped windsurfers break the 40-knot (47mph) speed barrier.

Owning the equipment is not cheap if bought new, however, good used stuff is out there in plentiful supply. When considering buying used gear keep in mind that the sail and rig are the "engine" and therefore the most important items.

Even an ugly board can outperform a new one if the sails are better or equal. Look for signs of excessive wear on the cloth like abrasions, cuts, repairs and stretched or threadbare seams. The two most important things to remember are that salt water rots everything and that design innovation is constant, so don't invest your money in anything that is too old.

Sailing sites vary in their appeal. Some sites, like Hookipa on Maui, are world-renowned for their huge waves and high winds. Hookipa is widely regarded as the best wave sailing in the world, and as such is regarded as the epicentre for progressive windsurfing, allowing expert sailors to sail full speed into the huge waves and shoot as high as 30 feet (9m) into the air and then ride the waves on the way back in!

Another great sailing site is the Columbia River Gorge in Oregon, where the wind roars up to 60 mph (96kph) up the river against a current heading the other way. The strong current and wind work together to create huge rolling waves, which attract thousands of sailors in the late summer each year. Other heavily visited sites include the Canary Islands, Southern France, Southern Spain, Western Australia and the Caribbean.

The great thing about windsurfing is that all you need is water, wind, and a board. The fun is just part of the deal. Just about anyone who can swim can windsurf, but you can just wear a life jacket if you're not that confident.

You will need instruction to start with but with a good technique you will find it is remarkably easy to do once you know the basics. It is a common mistake to think that you need to be strong to take part; there is a famous windsurfing proverb that if you need to be strong you are doing it wrong.

Once you have learned how to get up and ride, the trip from big board to short board windsurfing isn't long—it just takes some time, patience, and a little perseverance.

BORNE ON THE FOUR WINDS. CLOCKWISE (FROM NEAR RIGHT): RICH FOSTER; JOSH STONE; FRANCISCO GOYA (ALL PICTURED IN MAUI, HAWAII).

INDEX